Dramascripts
Billy Liar

WILLIS HALL AND KEITH WATERHOUSE

With notes and activities by
JOHN O'CONNOR

Thomas Nelson & Sons Ltd
Nelson House
Mayfield Road
Walton-on-Thames
Surrey KT12 5PL
United Kingdom

ı(T)P® Thomas Nelson is an International Thomson Company
ı(T)P® is used under licence

Designed and produced by Bender Richardson White
Typesetting by Malcolm Smythe
Cover illustration by Dave Grimwood
Black and white illustrations by John James
Printed by L. Rex Printing Co. Ltd., China

This edition published by Thomas Nelson & Sons Ltd 1998
ISBN 0 – 17 – 432549 – 5
9 8 7 6 5 4 3 2 1
01   00   99   98   97

CONTENTS

SERIES EDITOR'S INTRODUCTION

Dramascripts is an exciting series of plays especially chosen for students in the lower and middle years of secondary school. The titles range from the best in modern writing to adaptations of classic texts such as *A Christmas Carol* and *Silas Marner*.

Dramascripts can be read or acted purely for the enjoyment and stimulation that they provide; however, each play in the series also offers all the support that pupils need in working with the text in the classroom:

- **Introduction** – this offers important background information and explains something about the ways in which the play came to be written.
- **Script** – this is clearly set out in ways that make the play easy to handle in the classroom.
- **Notes** explain references that pupils might not understand, and language points that are not obvious.
- **Activities** – at the end of scenes, acts or sections – give pupils the opportunity to explore the play more fully. Types of activity include: discussion, writing, hot-seating, improvisation, acting, freeze-framing, story-boarding and artwork.
- **Looking Back at the Play** – this section has further activities for more extended work on the play as a whole with emphasis on characters, plots, themes and language.

A PRODUCTION NOTE BY THE AUTHORS

Taken at its face value, *Billy Liar* could be produced as a simple comedy about a boy who tells lies. There is, however, much more in it than this and the rewarding production will be the one that realises the strong dramatic theme which lies below the surface. Beneath the comedy runs the story of an imaginative youth fighting to get out of his complacent, cliché-ridden background. The director should not regard Billy as being a freak or a buffoon; the life of fantasy which he lives exists in most people but perhaps Billy's fantasies are nearer to the surface than most. The snatches of fantasy-life which are seen in the play should be directed for reality rather than comedy, and with subtlety rather than with the heavy hand which would take it dangerously near to farce. A production in which Billy is directed purely for laughs in the first two acts will find its audience unprepared to accept the serious content of the third act when Billy, for a time, sheds his final skins of make-believe.

Although Billy is the central character, his importance in the play can be seen only in contrast to his stolid family, and so it is important that his father, his mother and his grandmother should be seen as real persons and not as feeds. Similarly with the three girls it is necessary that Barbara and Rita should not be caricatures but should, in fact, be as real as Liz. On first reading of the text it will be seen that many of the lines are very funny – it must be appreciated however that the same lines are carefully naturalistic. It is this naturalism that the director should aim for in production. It may help the director to read the original novel on which the play was based.

Billy must remember that although he is very different from the rest of the family he is still a member of it. He has the family accent and the family mannerisms. Even when falling into fantasy his accent should not change all that much. For example, in the officer fantasy in Act Three, Billy will find that he will get a better effect by being a northern boy trying to imitate officer-class accents than by being the accomplished actor giving a skilful imitation of an officer. Billy will find that the over-all balance of the play hangs largely upon himself and it will be up to him to carry over the difficult transition of the play from Act Two to Act Three. It is important therefore that Billy's early fantasy scenes are not played as a kind of vaudeville act in an attempt to get as many laughs as possible. Billy must always remember that the purpose of all his fantasy scenes is to give the audience a key to what is going on in his mind.

Geoffrey is a more complex person than the blustering character who appears in Act One. The actor playing Geoffrey might find it helpful to study first the scene in Act Two in which Geoffrey tries to make some contact with Billy; he could then build up the character from this point rather than superimpose this facet of Geoffrey's character on a standard blustering performance. The word 'bloody' – which Geoffrey uses repeatedly – may give some trouble if it is used as an expletive and not as an unconscious punctuation mark in Geoffrey's dialogue. In the case of some amateur societies where the use of the word at all is likely to give offence, the authors give permission for it to be deleted completely – but not for the substitution of euphemisms such as 'ruddy', 'blooming', etc.

Alice is probably the least difficult of the characters to assess. She is a simple uncomplicated woman who has set her values many years ago and never re-examines them, not even in the most extraordinary circumstances. In her evaluation of other people's character she can see no further than the externals – personal appearance, manner of speech, etc. But it will be found that the role of Alice is very important for she is, so to speak, the hub of the circle of people we see in this play. All the arguments revolve around her; nothing takes place in the play that wil not affect her in one way or another. Alice, for all her soft-centred self-indulgent outlook is in fact a strong woman and should be cast as such.

Florence is a role which could easily tempt an actress to play a comic cameo without reference to the play at large. Little of Florence's dialogue is sparked off by other characters; she spends most of her time rambling to herself. This is not to say, however, that Florence does not react to what is going on around her. We must feel all the time that she belongs in the family and we should get the impression that she hears a great deal more than she appears to do. We must not get the impression that her day-dreams bear any similarity to Billy's fantasies, for when Florence goes into musings they are confined only to the hard realities of her past.

Barbara, although on one level a stolid, bovine character, is in her own way a fantasist just as much as Billy, for she lives in a woman's magazine world of thatched cottages and tweedy pipe-smoking heroes. Her reaction to Rita arises not too much out of jealousy at a rival as out of revulsion at having to face a side of life not normally on view through her rose-coloured spectacles.

Rita is a difficult character to play in that she has been written deliberately on one note, and a high note at that. The fact is that Rita is a simple, extrovert girl who does not change radically in any given situation. The way in which the actress playing this part should use her skill is in reproducing as accurately as possible the raucous irreverence of this type of working-class girl.

Liz, as can easily be seen, is the character closest to Billy in outlook and temperament. In spite of what we hear about her habits of flitting off from time to time she is not in any way a fey character, but has a down-to-earth quality which she tries to transmit to Billy. Although economically a member of the same class as Billy and his family, she has an outlook transcending its narrow boundaries and lower middle-class traits are not as apparent in her. The most important thing about Liz is that she should radiate warmth and generosity; but in playing her scene with Billy she should remember – as indeed Billy should remember – that this is a scene not about two people in love but two people who are trying to get love from each other.

Arthur is more than a feed for Billy. An ample study

of the part will reveal that there is a strong character change in Arthur as the play progresses. He begins in sympathy with Billy and his ideas but, lacking Billy's majestic sweep of vision, he grows jealous and impatient as the play moves along.

The characters in *Billy Liar* – with the exception of working-class Rita – come from a lower middle-class background in an industrial town. They should not have the broad 'Ee bah goom' accents of a mill town, mining town, or other closed northern community, but the simple broad accents of the provinces.

The lighting of the play is very important, especially in the third act. The lighting follows two conventions: the living-room is lit with complete naturalism – standard lamps, overhead light, etc.; but Billy's garden scene in Act Three, where the only natural light is that from the street lamp, gives the producer the opportunity to use his lighting to underline Billy's escape into a world of fantasy. The best effect, when Billy is discovered alone in the garden, is probably to start the scene in the naturalistic evening light of the garden and then, as Billy begins his 'officers and gentlemen' soliloquy, to diminish the lighting gradually until, when we come to the Last Post, Billy is standing in the light of a single spot.

The large set of living-room, hall and garden may pose something of a problem on smaller stages. In such cases it is suggested that the garden scenes be played on the bare stage in front of the living-room, and the garden seat dispensed with. The lighting, of course, should be appropriately changed.

A sample set of the play Billy Liar

THE CHARACTERS

GEOFFREY FISHER

ALICE FISHER, HIS WIFE

BILLY FISHER, THEIR SON

FLORENCE BOOTHROYD, ALICE FISHER'S MOTHER

ARTHUR CRABTREE

BARBARA

RITA

LIZ

BILLY LIAR
ACT 1

T he set consists of a living-room, entrance hall and a section of the garden of GEOFFREY FISHER'S house. It is a typical lower middle-class detached house in an industrial town in the north of England. To the left of the stage is the garden containing a small garden seat. The entrance to the house from the garden leads directly into the hallway with stairs going up to the bedrooms. Through the hallway is the living-room where most of the action of the play takes place. There is also a door in the living room right, leading into the kitchen. The room is furnished with an uncut moquette three-piece suite and a dining-room suite in dark oak. The furniture is quite new, but in dreadful taste – as are also the plaster ornaments and the wall plaques with which the room is over-dressed. Above the fireplace is the usual collection of family photographs on the mantelpiece and above the mantelpiece is a large brass-studded circular mirror. The room also contains a cheap and flashy cocktail cabinet, a large television set and also a sideboard with two cupboards.

As the curtain rises we discover FLORENCE BOOTHROYD sitting on the couch. She is ALICE FISHER'S mother, an old lady in her eighties, who finds it impossible to accustom herself to the modern way of life. She continually talks to herself and when she cannot be heard her lips continue to move. She is in the habit of addressing her remarks to inanimate objects. At the moment she is going through the contents of her large handbag. The handbag is open on her knees and as she takes out

lower middle-class detached house *A typical house lived in by people with reasonably well-paid manual jobs or who ran small businesses as Billy's father does.*

an uncut moquette three-piece suite *A sofa and armchairs covered in a thick velvety fabric, popular at that time (mid 1950s).*

in dreadful taste *The Fishers have no appreciation of 'style' in furnishings or decoration. One example of this is their 'flashy cocktail cabinet' – a cupboard with a glass front for the storage, and display, of drinks.*

wall plaques *These are ornaments which are fixed to the wall, such as flying ducks made of plaster.*

each object she examines it and then puts it down on the couch beside her, making a neat display. She has already taken out a few odd possessions and, at the moment, she is holding her old-age pension book. She addresses the sideboard.

FLORENCE   I don't know . . . They haven't stamped my book now . . .   1
They haven't sent it up. It should have gone up last week
but they haven't sent it up. *(She puts down the pension book
and takes a white hospital appointment card from her handbag.)*
That's not right either. Doctor Blakemore? I've never seen
Doctor Blakemore. Which is Doctor Blakemore? I bet it's
that black man. Else it's the lady doctor. I'm not seeing her.
Tuesday? They know I never go on Tuesdays. I've never
been on Tuesday yet. Doctor Thorpe said . . .

It comes to her that she is alone in the room. Putting down the   10
handbag she rises and crosses slowly and flat-footed to the
sideboard. She attempts to open the right-hand cupboard but,
discovering it is locked, returns to the couch and again takes up
her handbag.

He's as bad. And she encourages him. He lives in that bed.
(Noting the appointment card on the couch she picks it up.) And
where's that crêpe bandage they were going to get me? *(She
puts down the card.)* What's he always keep it locked up for,
anyroad? There's neither sense nor reason in that. And she
never tells you anything.   20

ALICE FISHER, GEOFFREY'S wife, enters from the kitchen. She

inanimate objects *'things which are not alive' (such as chairs, ornaments or the sideboard)*

They haven't stamped my book *The Post Office staff have not stamped Florence's pension book (to show that she has collected her money for that week).*

I bet it's that black man *Florence is of a generation who took some adjusting to the developing multi-cultural society that is the norm today.*

crêpe *A thin white crinkled fabric (bandages can be made from this); usually pronounced* **crayp.**

is a woman in her middle forties. Both ALICE and her husband have had working-class upbringings, but GEOFFREY'S success as a garage owner has moved them up into this new stratum of society. At the moment ALICE is caught up in the normal day-to-day rush of breakfast-time. She is speaking to her husband who is in the kitchen.

ALICE   Well, you do what you think fit, Geoffrey. Do what you like – it's no good me saying anything. But I know what I'd do. He still owes you for that last job you did for him.   **30**

ALICE crosses the room towards the hall, ignoring her mother who speaks to her as she passes.

FLORENCE   Who's Doctor Blakemore? Which one is that, then? Is that the one you went to?

ALICE   *(Entering the hall she calls up the stairs.)* It's time we were having you down, my lad. That bedroom clock's not fast, you know. It's half-past nine turned.

ALICE turns and re-enters the living-room.

FLORENCE   I'm not seeing Blakemore. I shan't go. I shall stop at home.

ALICE   If they say you've got to see him – you've got to see him,   **40** Mother. It's no good arguing. That's all there is to it.

GEOFFREY FISHER enters from the kitchen. He is a tall man in his early fifties. He is carrying a few invoices and, crossing and seating himself in an armchair, he begins to go through them.

FLORENCE   They caused all that bother on the buses in Birmingham. And Egypt. Mau-Mau. I make no wonder Eden's always so

---

Egypt *This is a reference to the Suez Crisis of 1956 when the Egyptian leader, Nasser, closed the Suez Canal; this led to an invasion by Israeli and Anglo-French forces.*

Mau-Mau *A guerrilla movement which operated in Africa 1952–60 with the aim of ending British colonial rule in Kenya.*

	badly. And him upstairs. He's just as bad. I think it's time his father talked to him. I don't know why he puts up with it. I can't understand why he lets him carry on like that.	
GEOFFREY	*(Looking up from the invoices he speaks to ALICE. In his speech he uses the adjective 'bloody' so frequently that it becomes completely meaningless.)* It's all right you talking, Alice, you don't understand. I've got no bloody choice. I can't turn work away. + Because he	50
ALICE	I've said what I've got to say. I'm not saying anything. I'm keeping out of it.	
FLORENCE	They let him carry on just as he likes. I wouldn't. I'd see to him.	
GEOFFREY	Where's his bloody lordship, then?	
FLORENCE	I'd tell her. She lets him lead her on. She wants to go up to him with a wet dish-cloth and wring it over his face. That'll get him up.	60
GEOFFREY	He wants a bloody good hiding.	
FLORENCE	. . . that'd move him . . .	
ALICE	I've shouted him three times.	
FLORENCE	. . . that'd shift him . . .	
GEOFFREY	It's every morning alike.	
FLORENCE	. . . he'd have to get up then.	
GEOFFREY	You let him do just as he likes!	

I make no wonder Eden's always so badly *'I'm not surprised Eden's always ill.' Sir Anthony Eden was British Prime Minister from 1955 until his retirement due to ill health in 1957.*

his bloody lordship *A sarcastic expression which implies that someone is 'behaving like a lord, expecting to be waited upon'.*

ALICE	*(Takes up the poker and a small shovel from the fireplace and crosses into the hall and calls up the stairs.)* Billy! . . . Billy! *(She bangs the poker against the shovel.)* I shan't tell you again. If I come up there you'll know about it! I suppose you know what time it is! Your boiled egg's stone cold and I'm not cooking another.	70
FLORENCE	She lets him do just as he likes.	
GEOFFREY	Go up to him. Go up and kick him out. He's bloody idle!	
	ALICE returns into the living-room and places the poker and shovel back into the fireplace.	
ALICE	It's all right you sitting there. You don't need to talk. You haven't emptied them ashes yet.	80
FLORENCE	She wants to go up to him. I would. *(She is now returning the objects to her handbag and pauses when she comes to the appointment card.)* It's a mystery to me about that crêpe bandage. I know I had it. It's in this house somewhere.	
GEOFFREY	You can't put anything down in this house. Not without somebody bloody shifting it. And who keeps taking my invoices out of that vase? Somebody bloody does.	
FLORENCE	He ought to see that window's properly locked every night. He never bolts that back door properly. It wants doing.	90
	BILLY FISHER begins to come down the bedroom stairs. He is nineteen years old and slightly built. He is wearing an old raincoat over his pyjamas. He is smoking a cigarette.	
ALICE	Is that him? He's stirred himself at last, then. I'll see what his breakfast is doing.	
	ALICE goes out to the kitchen as BILLY reaches the foot of the stairs. BILLY takes the morning paper from behind the door and enters the living-room.	
FLORENCE	She lets him do just as he likes.	

BILLY	*(Reading aloud from the paper.)* Cabinet Changes Imminent.	100
GEOFFREY	Yes, and you'll be bloody imminent if you don't start getting up on a morning.	
BILLY	Good morning, Father.	
GEOFFREY	Never mind bloody good mornings. It's bloody afternoon more like. If you think your mother's got nothing better to do than go round cooking six breakfasts every morning you've got another think coming.	
FLORENCE	She lets him do what he wants.	
BILLY	*(Ignoring his father he turns and bows, acting out the situation to his grandmother.)* Your servant, ma'am.	110
GEOFFREY	And you stop that bloody game. I'm talking to you. You're bloody hopeless. And you can start getting bloody well dressed before you come down in the morning.	
FLORENCE	He wants to burn that raincoat. He wants to burn it. Sling it on the fire-back. Then he'll have to get dressed whether or no.	
BILLY	I gather that he who would burn the raincoat is Father and he who should get dressed of a morning is my good self. Why do you always address all your remarks to the sideboard, Grandmother?	120
GEOFFREY	*(Almost rising from his chair.)* Here, here, here! Who do you

Cabinet Changes Imminent *Billy is constantly acting out different roles, from films he has seen in the cinema. Here he is the businessman interested in politics.*

Your servant, ma'am *Now Billy behaves like a gentleman from a Jane Austen novel.*

I gather that he who would burn the raincoat . . . *Billy is using the language of a pedantic (over-precise) school-teacher to mock Florence's confused speech. He does a similar thing with his father shortly afterwards ('Who are you having gallivanting around, then?') and again with his grandmother on page 8.*

think you're bloody talking to? You're not out with your daft mates now. And what time did you get in last night? If it was night. This bloody morning, more like.

ALICE enters from the kitchen.

BILLY	I really couldn't say. 'Bout half-past eleven, quarter to twelve. Good morning, Mother.
GEOFFREY	More like one o'clock, with your bloody half-past eleven! Well, you can bloody well start coming in of a night-time. I'm not having you gallivanting round at all hours, not at your bloody age.
BILLY	Who are you having gallivanting around, then?
GEOFFREY	And I'm not having any of your bloody lip. I'll tell you that, for a start.
ALICE	What were you doing down at Foley Bottoms at nine o'clock last night?
BILLY	Who says I was down at Foley Bottoms?
ALICE	Never mind who says, or who doesn't say. That's got nothing to do with it. You were there – somebody saw you. And it wasn't that Barbara you were with, either.
FLORENCE	He wants to make up his mind who he is going with.
GEOFFREY	He knocks about with too many lasses. He's out with a different one every night. He's like a bloody lass himself.
BILLY	Well, you want to tell whoever saw me to mind their own fizzing business.

130

— Sarcasm

140

gallivanting *'running around enjoying yourself'*

fizzing *Billy and his friend Arthur use a variety of euphemisms in place of swear-words (where Geoffrey would say 'bloody'). See elsewhere in the play e.g.,* **maring calendars** *(page 19),* **a naffing crêpe bandage** *(page 20), a* **cowing sight more** *(page 22),* **flaming Duxbury's** *(page 22) and* **stinking oranges** *(page 26). In a similar way, Billy tells Arthur to* **rot off** *(page 23).*

ALICE	It is our business – and don't you be so cheeky. You're not old enough for that.
FLORENCE	If she's coming for her tea this afternoon she wants to tell her. If she doesn't I will.
BILLY	I suppose that she who's coming for her tea is Barbara and she who wants to tell her is Mother and . . .
ALICE	I've told you – shut up. I'm going to tell her, don't you fret yourself. You've never played fair with that girl. Carrying on. I'm surprised she bothers with you. You shouldn't mess her about like that. One and then the other. That's no way to carry on. I know where you'll finish up – you'll finish up with none of them – that's where you'll finish up.
GEOFFREY	He'll finish up on his bloody ear-hole. I'm not having him staying out half the night. Not at his age. He's not old enough. He'll wait till he's twenty-one before he starts them bloody tricks. I've told him before, he can start coming in of a night or else go and live somewhere else.
BILLY	Perhaps I will do.
ALICE	*(Ignoring him.)* I can't understand that Barbara – why she does bother with you. Are you supposed to be getting engaged to her or aren't you?
GEOFFREY	He doesn't know who he's bloody getting engaged to.
FLORENCE	He wants to make his mind up.
ALICE	*(Ignoring GEOFFREY and FLORENCE.)* Because she's not like these others, you know. That time I saw you in the arcade with her she looked respectable to me. Not like that Liz or

150

160

170

DISCUSSION: The story, *Billy Liar*, is about a young man who lives partly in a fantasy world. Discuss as a class any other stories you know in which people make-believe.

DISCUSSION: What are your first impressions of Billy? What would he be like to live with?

whatever her name is. That scruffy one you reckoned to be going with. Her in that mucky skirt. Do you ever see anything of her still?

GEOFFREY He sees so many bloody lasses he doesn't know who he does see.

[handwritten: Billy 3rd person talking to him]

FLORENCE He wants to make his mind up – once and for all. He wants to make his mind up who he is going with.

BILLY I haven't seen Liz for three months.

ALICE Well, who were you with then? Down at Foley Bottoms?   180
Last night?

BILLY Rita.

GEOFFREY Who the bloody hell's Rita?

FLORENCE She wants to see that he makes his mind up.

ALICE I shall tell Barbara this afternoon – I shall tell her, make no mistake about that.

[handwritten: degrading, disparage]

GEOFFREY He's never satisfied with what he has got – that's his bloody trouble. He never has been. It's ever since he left school. It's ever since he took that job – clerking. Clerking for that undertaker – what kind of a bloody job's that?   190

BILLY Perhaps I might not be doing it much longer.

GEOFFREY You what?

ALICE What do you mean?

BILLY I've been offered a job in London.

GEOFFREY *(Turning away in disgust.)* Don't talk bloody wet.

ALICE How do you mean? A job in London? What job in London?

clerking *'working as a clerk'; 'doing low-grade office work'*

undertaker *Someone who organises funerals.*

BILLY	*(Taking a crumpled envelope from his raincoat pocket.)* What I say, I've been offered a job in London. Script-writing.
GEOFFREY *Crinkle*	Bloody script-writing.
ALICE	What script-writing? 200
GEOFFREY	Script-writing! He can't write his bloody name so you can read it. Who'd set him on?
BILLY	*(Proudly.)* Danny Boon.
ALICE	Danny who?
BILLY	*(Going into a slow, exasperated explanation.)* I told you before. Boon. Danny Boon. I told you. He was on at the Empire the week before last. When he was there I told you. I went to see him. I went to his dressing-room. I took him some of my scripts. Well, he's read them. He's read them and he likes them. And he's sent me this letter. He's offered me a 210 job in London. Script-writing. Danny Boon. The comedian. He's been on television.
FLORENCE	*(Addressing the television.)* It's always boxing; boxing and horse shows.
ALICE	*(Ignoring her.)* Danny Boon? I don't remember ever seeing him.
GEOFFREY	No, and neither does anybody else. It's another of his tales. Danny Boon! He's made him up.
ALICE	What kind of a job?
BILLY	I've told you. Script-writing. 220

(handwritten annotation: The really)

DISCUSSION: In pairs. check that you are following Billy's love-life. Who are Billy's girl-firends? What is his relationship with each one?

ACTING: In groups of four, act out page 10. Bring out Billy's exasperation in the speech beginning, 'I told you before . . ', with all its short sentences, Alice's bewilderment, Geoffrey's bad temper and Florence's ramblings.

GEOFFREY	It's like all these other tales he comes home with. He can't say two words to anybody without it's a bloody lie. And what's he been telling that woman in the fish shop about me having my leg off? Do I look as though I've had my leg off?
BILLY	It wasn't you. It was Barbara's uncle. She gets everything wrong – that woman in the fish shop.
ALICE	You'll have to stop all this making things up, Billy. There's no sense in it at your age. We never know where we are with you. I mean, you're too old for things like that now. **230**
BILLY	*(Displaying the letter.)* Look – all right then. I've got the letter – here. He wants me to go down to see him. In London. To fix things up. I'm going to ring up this morning and give them my notice.
ALICE	You can't do things like that, Billy. You can't just go dashing off to London on spec.
GEOFFREY	*(Disparagingly.)* He's not going to no bloody London. It's them that'll be ringing him up, more like. You'll get the sack – I'll tell you what you'll get. What time are you supposed to be going in there this morning, anyroad? **240**
BILLY	I'm not. It's my Saturday off this week.
GEOFFREY	You said that last bloody week. That's three bloody weeks in a row.
BILLY	I got mixed up.
GEOFFREY	I've no patience with you. *(He places the invoices in his pocket and rises from his chair.)* Anyway, I've got some work to do if you haven't.

---

on spec *'taking the chance that something good will turn up'*

disparagingly *'with contempt'; running Billy down*

ALICE	Are you going in towards town, Geoffrey?
GEOFFREY	I'm going in that direction.
ALICE	You can drop me off. I'm going down as far as the shops. 　250
GEOFFREY	I can if you're not going to be all bloody day getting ready. I'm late now.
ALICE	*(Crossing towards the hall.)* I'm ready now. I've only to slip my coat on.
	ALICE goes out into the hall and puts on a coat which is hanging on the rack. GEOFFREY turns to BILLY.
GEOFFREY	And you can get your mucky self washed – and get bloody dressed. And keep your bloody hands off my razor else you'll know about it.
FLORENCE	*(Raising her voice.)* Is she going past Driver's? 'Cause there's 　260 that pork pie to pick up for this afternoon's tea.
	ALICE re-enters the living-room.
ALICE	I'm ready. I'll call in for that pie. *(To BILLY.)* Your breakfast's on the kitchen table. It'll be clap-cold by now.
GEOFFREY	*(Crossing towards the door. He turns for a final sally at BILLY.)* And you can wash them pots up when you've finished. Don't leave it all for your mother.
ALICE	I shan't be above an hour, Mother.
	ALICE and GEOFFREY go out through the hall and into the 　270 *garden. BILLY goes into the kitchen.*
FLORENCE	I shouldn't be left on my own. She's not said anything now about the insurance man. I don't know what to give him if

clap-cold *'completely cold'*

the insurance man *A door-to-door collector of weekly life insurance premiums.*

he comes.

ALICE and GEOFFREY are moving down the garden.

GEOFFREY   I'm only going as far as the lane, you know, I don't know why you can't get the bloody bus.

ALICE and GEOFFREY exeunt. BILLY re-enters from the kitchen. He is carrying a cup and a teapot.

BILLY   I can't eat that egg. It's stone cold.

FLORENCE   There's too much waste in this house. It's all goodness just 280
thrown down the sink. We had to eat it. When I was his age we couldn't leave nothing. If we didn't eat it then it was put out the next meal. When we had eggs, that was. We were lucky to get them. You had to make do with what there was. Bread and dripping.

BILLY   *(Sitting down he pours himself a cup of tea.)* Do you want a cup of tea?

FLORENCE   And if you weren't down at six o'clock of a morning you didn't get that.

BILLY   *(He drinks and grimaces.)* They don't drink tea in London at 290
this time of a morning. It's all coffee. That's what I'll be doing this time next week.

FLORENCE   Sundays was just the same. No lying-in then.

BILLY and his grandmother are now in their own separate dreamworlds.

BILLY   Sitting in a coffee-bar. Espresso. With a girl. Art student. Duffle-coat and dirty toe-nails. I discovered her the night before. Contemplating suicide.

Sitting in a coffee bar . . .*This is another of Billy's fantasies derived from the cinema: a vision of fashionable coffee-bar London – Billy would never have tasted Espresso coffee.*

FLORENCE	If you had a job in them days you had to stick to it. You couldn't get another.

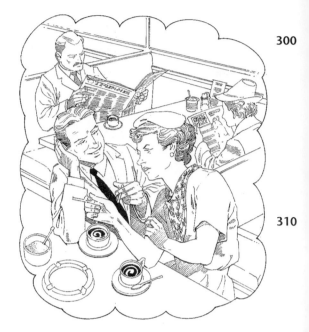

300

BILLY	*(Addressing his imaginary companion.)* Nothing is as bad as it seems, my dear. Less than a week ago my father felt the same as you. Suicidal. He came round after the operation and looked down where his legs should have been. Nothing.

310

FLORENCE   We couldn't go traipsing off to London or anywhere else. If we got as far as Scarborough we were lucky.

BILLY   Just an empty space in the bed. Well, he'll never be World Champion now. A broken man on two tin legs.

320

BILLY slowly levers himself out of his chair and limps slowly and painfully around the room leaning heavily against the furniture.

FLORENCE   *(Addressing BILLY in the third person.)* He's not right in the head.

BILLY realises he is being watched and comes out of his fantasy.

traipsing off *An expression used when you disapprove of a person going somewhere.*

I wouldn't care, but it makes me poorly watching him.

BILLY   *(Rubbing his leg and by way of explanation.)* Cramp.

FLORENCE   He wants to get his-self dressed.   330

Playing @ being northeners

ARTHUR CRABTREE enters the garden and approaches the front door. He is about the same age as BILLY. He is wearing flannels, a sports coat and a loud checked shirt. He pushes the door-bell which rings out in two tones in the hall.

Oxford Brummen men

(As BILLY crosses to answer the bell.) He shouldn't be going to the door dressed like that.

BILLY opens the door and, together with ARTHUR, goes into a routine – their usual way of greeting each other. ARTHUR holds up an imaginary lantern and peers into an imaginary darkness.

ARTHUR   *(In a thick north-country accent.)* There's trouble up at the   340
mill.

BILLY   *(Also in a thick north-country accent.)* What's afoot, Ned *he uses*
Leather? Is ~~Willy Arkwright~~ smashing up my looms again?

Pissing around

ARTHUR   It's the men! They'll not stand for that lad of yours down from Oxford and Cambridge.

BILLY   They'll stand for him and lump it. There's allus been an Oldroyd at Oldroyd's mill and there allus will be.

ARTHUR   Nay, Josiah! He's upsetting them with his fancy college ways and they'll have none of it. They're on the march! They're coming up the drive!   350

? **flannels** *trousers made of a woollen fabric (smart wear for work at that time)*

(in a thick north-country accent) *Billy and Arthur improvise the kind of dialogue heard in certain plays and films set in 19th Century northern mill towns.*

They'll not stand for that lad of yours . . . *The stories often involved a clash between the young son, who had returned educated, and the traditional community. This parallels Billy with his grammar school education, now mocking his Yorkshire roots.*

Fcuk   *Fun / Fun*   *FCUT*   15

BILLY  Into the house, Ned *is sod* and bar the door! We've got to remember our Sal's condition.

They enter together and march into the living-room where they both dissolve into laughter.

·Fun

FLORENCE Carrying on and making a commotion. It's worse than Bedlam. Carrying on and all that noise. They want to make less noise, the pair of them.

ARTHUR Good morning, Mrs Boothroyd.

FLORENCE He wants to make less noise and get his-self dressed.

BILLY Do you want a cup of tea, Arthur? I'm just having my breakfast.   360

ARTHUR You rotten idle crow! Some of us have done a day's work already, you lazy get.

BILLY Why aren't you at work now?

ARTHUR Why aren't you at rotten work, that's why I'm not at work. Come to see where you are. They're going bonkers at the office. You never turned in last Saturday either.

BILLY Isn't it my Saturday off this week?

ARTHUR You know rotten well it isn't.

FLORENCE *(Getting up from the couch.)* They're all idle. They're all the   370
same. They make me badly.

FLORENCE crosses the room and disappears up the stairs into the bedroom.

---

our Sal's condition *Sister Sal is pregnant. Another expression is 'in the family way': page 17.*

worse than Bedlam . . . *'Worse than the mad-house'. Bedlam was a famous lunatic asylum.*

lazy get *'get' is their version of 'git'.*

bonkers *'mad'*

BILLY	I could say I forgot and thought it was.
ARTHUR	You can hellers like. You said that last week.
BILLY	Tell them my grandad's had his leg off.
ARTHUR	You haven't got a rotten grandad. Anyroad, I can't tell them anything. I'm not supposed to have seen you. I've come up in my break. I'm supposed to be having my coffee. I'm not telling them anything. I'm having enough bother as it is **380** with our old lady. What with you and your lousy stories. Telling everybody she was in the family way. She's heard about it. She says she's going to come up here and see your father.
BILLY	Cripes, she can't do that! It was only last night I told him she'd just had a miscarriage. She's not supposed to be up yet.
ARTHUR	What the hell did you tell him that for?
BILLY	I hadn't any choice. My mother was going to send a present round for the baby. **390**
ARTHUR	The trouble with you, cocker, is you're just a rotten pathological liar. Anyway, you've done it this time. You've dropped yourself right in with not coming in this morning.

You can hellers like. *'Like hell, you can!' Compare 'Did she heckerslike!' on page 37 – 38.*

a miscarriage *'losing a baby'. If this were true, Arthur's mother would be still confined to bed.*

pathological liar *'lying is an illness with him'*

DISCUSSION: As a class discuss the main things that you have learned so far about Florence. What kinds of things occupy her mind? What advice would you give to an actress on how to play the character?

ACTING: In pairs, try reading the 'trouble up at the mill' dialogue in the 'thick north-country accent' required.

BILLY	I can get out of that. I'll think of some excuse.
ARTHUR	There's more to it than that, matey. Shadrack's been going through your postage book.
BILLY	When?
ARTHUR	This morning, when do you think? There's nearly three rotten quid short. All there is in the book is one stinking lousy rotten threepenny stamp and he says he gave you two **400** pound ten stamp money on Wednesday.
BILLY	Fizzing hell! Has he been through the petty cash as well?
ARTHUR	Not when I left. No. Why, have you been fiddling that as well?
BILLY	No, no . . . I haven't filled the book up, though.
ARTHUR	And he was going on about some calendars – I don't know what he meant.
BILLY	*(Crossing to the sideboard.)* I do.
	BILLY takes a small key from his raincoat pocket and opens the right-hand cupboard. As he does so a pile of large envelopes fall **410** *out on to the carpet followed by a few odds and ends.*
	There you are, Tosh, two hundred and sixty of the bastards.
ARTHUR	What?
BILLY	Maring calendars.
ARTHUR	*(Crosses and picks up an envelope from the floor.)* What do you want with two rotten hundred and sixty calendars?
	(He reads the address on the front of the envelope.)

postage book *Billy is given money each week with which to buy stamps that are then supposed to be put in a book and used when needed.*

Tosh *A friendly term of address like 'mate'. Arthur calls Billy 'tosher' (page 23).*

'The Mother Superior, The Convent of the Sacred Heart!'

He tears open the envelope and takes out a long, wall calendar illustrated with a colourful painting of a kitten and a dog. He reads the inscription.   **420**

'Shadrack and Duxbury, Funeral Furnishers.' These are the firm's! 'Taste, Tact and Economy.' You skiving nit! You should have posted these last Christmas.

BILLY   Yes.

ARTHUR   Well, what are they doing in your sideboard cupboard?

BILLY   I never had enough stamps in the postage book.

ARTHUR   You think that postage money's part of your bloody wages, don't you?

He bends down and sorts through the pile of papers on the floor.   **430**

Why do you keep them in there?

BILLY   It's where I keep all my private things.

ARTHUR   (*Picking up a small package.*) Private things! A naffing crêpe bandage!

He throws down the package and picks up a piece of blue notepaper.

What's this then?

BILLY   (*Making a grab for the letter.*) Gerroff, man! Give us that here! That's personal!

ARTHUR   (*Evading BILLY's hand.*) What the hell are you writing to   **440** Godfrey Winn for?

BILLY   It's not me. It's my mother.

? skiving nit *Arthur accuses Billy of skiving.*

Godfrey Winn *This was a radio personality who presented a popular request programme, 'Housewives' Choice'*

ARTHUR	*(Reading the letter.)* 'Dear Sir, Just a few lines to let you know how much I enjoy 'Housewives' Choice' every day, I always listen no matter what I am doing, could you play *'Just a Song at Twilight'* for me.' That's a turn-up for the top-ten! She isn't half with it, your old lady! *(Reading.)* 'I don't suppose you get time to play everyone that writes to you, but this is my favourite song. You see my husband often used to sing it when we were a bit younger than we are **450** now. I will quite understand if you cannot play. Yours respectfully Mrs A. Fisher.' So why didn't you post this then?
BILLY	I couldn't be bothered. *(He makes a further attempt to grab the letter.)* Give us it here!
ARTHUR	*(Holding him off.)* 'P.S. My son also writes songs, but I suppose there is not much chance for him as he has not had the training. We are just ordinary folk.'
BILLY	*(Snatches the letter and tosses it into the cupboard.)* I'm not ordinary folk even if she is. *(He crams the envelopes* **460** *containing the calendars back into the cupboard.)* I keep trying to get rid of them. It was bad enough getting them out of the office.
ARTHUR	How long have they been here?
BILLY	Not long. I used to keep them in that coffin in the basement at work. You can't get rid of the fizzing things! It's like a bloody nightmare. They won't burn. I've tried tearing them up and pushing them down the lavatory – all they do is float.
ARTHUR	Makes no difference what you do with them. Duxbury's on **470** to you. He knows about them.

the top-ten *Music charts in the 1950s.*

with it *One of many terms, some still in use, to mean 'aware of fashion': others are 'cool', 'hip' and 'trendy'.*

BILLY	*(Stuffing the last of the calendars into the cupboard he locks the door.)* Oh well . . . so what. He knows what he can do with his calendars. I don't give a monkey's. I'm leaving. I've got another job.
ARTHUR	Leaving?
BILLY	I'm going to ring him up this morning and give him my notice.
ARTHUR	Yes, and we've heard that one before.
BILLY	No, straight up. I'm going to London.
ARTHUR	What as – road-sweeper?
BILLY	*(Grandiloquently.)* Ay road sweepah on the road – to fame! *(He returns to his normal voice.)* I've got that job with Danny Boon.
ARTHUR	You haven't!
BILLY	Yes – script-writer. Start next week.
ARTHUR	You jammy burk! Have you though, honest?
BILLY	Yeh – course I have. It's all fixed up. He sent me a letter. Asking me to work for him.
ARTHUR	What's he paying you?
BILLY	A cowing sight more that I get from Shadrack and flaming Duxbury's.
ARTHUR	What? Counting the postage?
BILLY	What's it to you? This is it for me, boy! Success! 'Saturday Night Spectacular!' 'Sunday Night at the Palladium!'

480

490

I don't give a monkey's *'I don't care.'* (polite version)

Grandiloquently *'over-dramatically and pompously'*

jammy burk *'lucky idiot'*

Play in London

Script by!

ARTHUR	Ta-ra-ra-raaa!
BILLY	Billy Fisher! Directed by!
ARTHUR	Ta-ra-ra-raaa!
BILLY	William Fisher! Produced by!
ARTHUR	Ta-ra-ra-raaa!
BILLY	William S. Fisher!
ARTHUR	Ta-ra-ra-raaa!

500

BILLY   A W.S. Fisher Presentation! 'Mr Fisher, on behalf of the British Television Industry, serving the needs of twenty million viewers, it gives me great pleasure to present you with this award, this evening, in recognition of the fact that you have been voted Television Script-writer of the Year – for the seventh year running.'

ARTHUR   *(Picking up a vase from the sideboard he places it in BILLY'S hands.)* Big-head.

510

BILLY   *(Returning the vase to the sideboard.)* Rot off. You wait and see.

ARTHUR   *(Taking a small bottle of tablets from his trouser pocket.)* So you won't be needing these now, then, will you?

BILLY   What's them?

ARTHUR   Passion pills. What I said I'd get for you.

BILLY   *(Taking the bottle incredulously.)* Let's have a look, mate. *(He opens the bottle and is about to swallow one of the tablets.)* What do they taste like?

520

'Saturday Night Spectacular!' 'Sunday Night at the London Palladium!' *Two popular television shows in the late 1950s.*

Passion pills *'aphrodisiacs'; pills to increase someone's sexual desire.*

ARTHUR	Here, go steady on, man! They'll give you the screaming ab-dabs.
BILLY	*(Returning the tablet to the bottle.)* How did you get hold of them?
ARTHUR	From a mate of mine who got demobbed. He brought them back from Singapore.
BILLY	I'll bet they're bloody aspirins.
ARTHUR	Do you want to bet? You want to ask this bloke, tosher.
BILLY	How many do you give them?
ARTHUR	Just one. Two two-and-nines at the Regal, a bag of chips and one of these and you're away. Who's it for anyway?
BILLY	Barbara . . . Bloody hell!
ARTHUR	What's up?
BILLY	She's supposed to be coming round this morning.
ARTHUR	I thought it was this afternoon? For her tea?
BILLY	*(Placing the bottle of tablets on the sideboard.)* No, I've got to see her first. Our old man'll go bald if he sees her before I've had a word with her. She thinks he's in the Merchant Navy.

> **They'll give you the screaming ab-dabs.** *'They'll drive you mad.'*
>
> **got demobbed** *'left the army'; was 'demobilised'*
>
> **two-and-nines at the Regal** *Seats costing two shillings and nine pence (about 14 pence today) at the local cinema.*

> **HOT-SEATING:** In groups of four, one person takes on the character of Alice. Ask her how she feels about the family. In particular, what does she mean by 'We are just ordinary folk.'?
>
> **HOT-SEATING:** Interview Billy about his ambitions. What does he see himself doing in ten years' time, for example?

ARTHUR	You what?
BILLY	(*Crossing hurriedly towards the hall.*) On petrol tankers. (*He indicates the tea-things.*) Shift them into the kitchen for me. Shan't be a tick.

540

BILLY *runs up the stairs in the hall and into his bedroom. ARTHUR picks up the teapot and goes into the kitchen. ARTHUR re-enters and crosses to the sideboard where he picks up the bottle of tablets. BILLY appears at the top of the stairs with his clothes in his hands. BILLY moves down the stairs and enters the living-room. ARTHUR replaces the tablets on the sideboard.*

ARTHUR	What time's she supposed to be coming?
BILLY	(*Dressing hastily.*) Quarter of an hour since. Where's them passion pills?

550

ARTHUR	On the sideboard. You're not going to slip her one this morning are you?

2× *mer* **BILLY** Why not? I'm pressed for time, man. I'm going out with Rita tonight.

ARTHUR	Well, what about your grandmother?
BILLY	Oh, she's spark out till dinner-time.
ARTHUR	I've lost track of your rotten sex life. Which one are you supposed to be engaged to, anyway?
BILLY	That's what they call an academic question.

560

ARTHUR	Well, you can't be engaged to both of them at once, for God's sake.
BILLY	Do you want to bet?

spark out *'flat out'; 'fast asleep'*

an academic question *Billy is using the wrong expression. An 'academic' question is one that doesn't have much relevance to everyday life. He simply means 'that's a difficult question'.*

ARTHUR	Crikey! Well, which of them's got the naffing engagement ring?
BILLY	Well, that's the trouble. That's partly the reason why Barbara's coming round this morning – if she did but know it. She's got it. I've got to get it off her. For Rita.
ARTHUR	What for?
BILLY	Ah, well . . . You see, she had it first – Rita. Only I got it from her to give to Barbara. Now she wants it back. I told her it was at the jeweller's – getting the stone fixed. There'll be hell to pay if she doesn't get it.

570

ARTHUR	The sooner you get to London the better.
BILLY	*(Tucking his shirt in his trousers and slipping on his jacket.)* Are you sure them passion pills'll work on Barbara? She's dead from the neck down.
ARTHUR	You haven't tried.
BILLY	Tried! Who hasn't tried! If you want to try you're welcome. All she does is sit and eat stinking oranges.

580

ARTHUR	What I can't work out is why you got engaged to her in the first place. What's wrong with Liz?
BILLY	Don't talk to me about Liz. I've not seen her for months. She's tooled off to Bradford or somewhere.
ARTHUR	Well, she's tooled back again then. I saw her this morning.
BILLY	What? Liz?
ARTHUR	Yeh – scruffy Lizzie. I bumped into her in Sheepgate. Mucky as ever. It's about time somebody bought her a new skirt.

 tooled off *'gone away'*

Barny

	BARBARA approaches the house. She is about nineteen years old, a large well-built girl in a tweed suit and flat-heeled shoes. She is carrying a large handbag. **590**
BILLY	Did she say anything about me?
ARTHUR	I didn't stop. Just said 'Hello'. I wouldn't be seen stood standing talking to that scruffy-looking bird.
	BARBARA rings the bell.
BILLY	That's Barbara! Where's them passion pills!
	BILLY crosses and taking the bottle from the sideboard he places it in his breast pocket. ARTHUR crosses towards the door.
ARTHUR	I'll have to get going, anyway. I'll get shot when I get back to work. I've been gone nearly half an hour now. **600**
BILLY	*(Crossing towards the door.)* Hang on a couple of minutes, man. Don't make it look too obvious! If she sees you going out and leaving her with me she'll be out of that door like a whippet.
ARTHUR	I'm late now!
BILLY	You can chat her up for a minute.
	BILLY crosses into the hall and opens the door to admit BARBARA.
	Hallo, darling!

no excitement.

BARBARA	*(Who uses endearments coldly and flatly.)* Hallo, pet. **610**
BILLY	*(Leading the way.)* Come through into the lounge.

?   **a tweed suit and flat-heeled shoes** *Barbara is dressed as a middle-aged person would dress at that time, in heavy unfashionable clothes.*

whippet *A small dog like a greyhound, used for racing.*

uses endearments coldly and flatly *There is no real emotion in her use of 'pet' and 'darling'.*

BARBARA	*(Following BILLY into the living-room.)* Hallo, Arthur.
	ARTHUR winks at her. BARBARA looks round the room.
	What a nice room!
	(She crosses to examine the cocktail cabinet.) Boring Comments
	What a beautiful cocktail cabinet!
BILLY	I made it. — lyer
	ARTHUR reacts to this statement.
BARBARA	How clever of you, sweet. I didn't know you could do woodwork. — gullible + stupid 620
BILLY	Oh yes, I made all the furniture. *(A pause and then, wildly.)* And the garage. — Smell a
	BARBARA looks around the room doubtfully.
ARTHUR	*(Coughs.)* It's time I was making a move, mate.
BARBARA	You're not going because of me, Arthur?
ARTHUR	No, I'm supposed to be at work. *(To BILLY.)* So long, Tosh!
BILLY	So long.
BARBARA	Bye! . . . Isn't your sister in, Billy?
ARTHUR	*(Stops short on his way to the door and turns.)* What bloody sister? ~ another lye 630
	BILLY, unnoticed by BARBARA, gesticulates to ARTHUR to leave. ARTHUR does so – hastily.
BILLY	Barbara, I'm glad you asked me that question. About my sister.

lounge *At the time, this was a new and fashionable term for a living-room.*

BARBARA	What is it?
BILLY	Sit down, darling. *(BARBARA sits on the couch.)* Darling, are you still coming to tea this afternoon?
BARBARA	Of course.
BILLY	Because there are some things I want to tell you.
BARBARA	What things, Billy?
BILLY	You know what you said the other night – about loving me? Even if I were a criminal.
BARBARA	Well?
BILLY	You said you'd still love me even if I'd murdered your mother.
BARBARA	*(Suspiciously.)* Well?
BILLY	I wonder if you'll still love me when you hear what I've got to say. You see – well, you know that I've got a fairly vivid imagination, don't you?
BARBARA	Well, you have to have if you're going to be a script-writer, don't you?
BILLY	Well, being a script-writer, I'm perhaps – at times – a bit inclined to let my imagination run away with me. As you know. *(BARBARA is even more aloof than usual.)* You see, the thing is, if we're going to have our life together – and that cottage – and little Billy and little Barbara and the lily pond and all that . . Well, there's some things we've got to get cleared up.
BARBARA	What things?
BILLY	Some of the things I'm afraid I've been telling you.
BARBARA	Do you mean you've been telling me lies?
BILLY	Well, not lies exactly . . . But I suppose I've been well, exaggerating some things. Being a script-writer . . . For

640

650

660

	instance, there's that business about my father. Him being a sea captain. On a petrol tanker.
BARBARA	You mean he's not on a petrol tanker?
BILLY	He's not even in the navy.
BARBARA	Well, what is he?
BILLY	He's in the removal business.
BARBARA	And what about him being a prisoner-of-war? And that tunnel? And the medal? Don't say that was all lies?
BILLY	Yes. *(BARBARA turns away abruptly.)* Are you cross?
BARBARA	No – not cross. Just disappointed. It sounds as though you were ashamed of your father.
BILLY	I'm not ashamed. I'm not – I'm not!
BARBARA	Otherwise why say he was a prisoner-of-war? What was he?
BILLY	A conscientious ob . . . *(He checks himself.)* He wasn't anything. He wasn't fit. He has trouble with his knee.
BARBARA	The knee he's supposed to have been shot in, I suppose.
BILLY	Yes. Another thing, we haven't got a budgie, or a cat. And I didn't make the furniture . . . Not all of it, anyway.
BARBARA	How many other lies have you been telling me?
BILLY	My sister.
BARBARA	Don't tell me you haven't got a sister.
BILLY	I did have. But she's dead. If you're still coming for your tea this afternoon they never talk about her.

670

680

BARBARA remains silent, her head still turned away.

A conscientious ob . . . *Billy is about to lie that his father was a conscientious objector (someone who refused to fight on grounds of conscience).*

You remind me of her . . . If you're not coming I'll understand . . I'm just not good enough for you, Barbara . . . If you want to give me the engagement ring back – I'll understand. **690**

BARBARA *(Turning towards him.)* Don't be cross with yourself, Billy. I forgive you.

BILLY *(Moving to kiss her.)* Darling . . .

BARBARA *(Moving away.)* But promise me one thing.

BILLY That I'll never lie to you again? *(BARBARA nods.)* I'll never lie to you again. Never, I promise . . . Darling, there is one thing. I have got a grannie.

BARBARA I believe you.

BILLY Only she's not blind. She's not very well, though. She's **700** upstairs. Sleeping. She might have to have her leg off.

BARBARA *(Kissing him.)* Poor darling.

BILLY *(Moving quickly towards the cocktail cabinet.)* Would you like a drink?

BARBARA Not now, pet.

BILLY *(Opening the cabinet.)* Port. To celebrate.

BARBARA All right. Well, just a tiny one.

BILLY I'm turning over a new leaf.

Unnoticed by BARBARA he pours the drink and taking a tablet from the 'passion pill' bottle, places it in her glass. He crosses **710** *with the glasses and sits beside her on the couch.*

That's yours darling.

BARBARA *(Sitting on the edge of the couch she sips the port.)* Let's talk about something nice.

BILLY Let's talk about our cottage.

30

BARBARA	Oh, I've seen the most marvellous material to make curtains for the living-room. Honestly, you'll love it. It's a sort of turquoise with lovely little squiggles like wine-glasses.

Dull

BILLY	Will it go with the yellow carpet?	
BARBARA	No, but it will go with the grey rugs.	720
BILLY	*(Taking her in his arms.)* I love you, darling.	
BARBARA	*(Moving away.)* I love you.	
BILLY	Do you? Really and truly?	
BARBARA	Of course I do.	
BILLY	Are you looking forward to getting married?	

BARBARA takes an orange from her handbag and peels it and eats it during the following dialogue.

BARBARA	I think about it every minute of the day.	
BILLY	Darling . . . *(He again attempts unsuccessfully to kiss her.)* Don't ever fall in love with anybody else.	730
BARBARA	Let's talk about our cottage.	

Dull

BILLY	*(Simulating a dreamy voice.)* What about our cottage?
BARBARA	About the garden. Tell me about the garden.

Dream

BILLY	We'll have a lovely garden. We'll have roses in it and daffodils and a lovely lawn with a swing for little Billy and little Barbara to play on. And we'll have our meals down by the lily pond in summer.

unlikely reality

BARBARA	Do you think a lily pond is safe? What if the kiddies wandered too near and fell in?

Similar to Author dialoge p 15 but this is not a game for barbara

simulating *'pretending'*

BILLY	We'll build a wall round it. No – no, we won't. We won't have a pond at all. We'll have an old well. An old brick well where we draw the water. We'll make it our wishing well. Do you know what I'll wish?	740
BARBARA	*(Shaking her head.)* No.	
BILLY	Tell me what you'll wish first.	
BARBARA	Oh, I'll wish that we'll always be happy. And always love each other. What will you wish?	
BILLY	Better not tell you.	
BARBARA	Why not, pet?	
BILLY	You might be cross.	750
BARBARA	Why would I be cross?	
BILLY	Oh, I don't know . . . You might think me too . . . well, forward. *(He glances at her face but can see no reaction.)* Barbara . . . ? Do you think it's wrong for people to have – you know, feelings?	
BARBARA	Not if they're genuinely in love with each other.	
BILLY	Like we are.	
BARBARA	*(Uncertainly.)* Yes.	
BILLY	Would you think it wrong of me to have – feelings?	
BARBARA	*(Briskly and firmly.)* I think we ought to be married first.	760
BILLY	*(Placing his hand on BARBARA'S knee.)* Darling . . .	
BARBARA	Are you feeling all right?	
BILLY	Of course, darling. Why?	
BARBARA	Look where your hand is.	
BILLY	Darling, don't you want me to touch you?	
BARBARA	*(Shrugging.)* It seems . . . indecent, somehow.	

BILLY	Are you feeling all right?
BARBARA	Yes, of course.
BILLY	How do you feel?
BARBARA	Contented.
BILLY	You don't feel . . . you know – restless?
BARBARA	No.
BILLY	Finish your drink.
BARBARA	In a minute *(She opens her handbag and offers it towards him.)* Have an orange.

BILLY snatching the bag from her, throws it down and oranges spill out across the floor.

BILLY	You and your bloody oranges!
BARBARA	*(Remonstratively.)* Billy ! . . . Darling!
BILLY	*(Placing his head on her shoulder.)* I'm sorry, darling. I've had a terrible morning.
BARBARA	Why? What's happened?
BILLY	Oh, nothing. The usual. Family and things. Just that I've got a headache.
BARBARA	I'm sorry, pet. You know, you ought to see a doctor.
BILLY	I've seen doctors – specialists – I've seen them all. All they could give me was a crêpe bandage. *(BARBARA, unimpressed, licks her fingers.)* You know, my darling, I think you have feelings, too. Deep down.
BARBARA	*(Examining her hands distastefully.)* Oooh, sticky paws!

770

780

790

remonstratively *'telling him off'*

33

BILLY   Wipe them on the cushion. *(He rises as a thought strikes him.)* You can go upstairs if you want. Use our bathroom.

BARBARA   Thank you.

BARBARA, picking up her handbag, crosses into the hall and goes upstairs. BILLY picks up her glass and crosses to the cocktail cabinet, where he pours out two more drinks. Taking the 'passion pills' from his pocket he adds two pills to BARBARA'S glass and then, on impulse, he adds the entire contents of the bottle into her glass. He is standing admiring the glass and its contents as the telephone rings in the hall. He places the glass on the table 800 *and crosses into the hall where he picks up the phone.*

BILLY   *LIE* *Down to reality* *Lie*

The Fisher residence? Can I help you? *(His manner changes.)* Oh, hullo, Mr. Duxbury. No, well, I'm sorry but I've had an accident. I was just leaving for work and I spilt this hot water down my arm. I had to get it bandaged . . . Oh, well, I think there's a very simple explanation for that, Mr Duxbury. You see, there's a lot of those figures that haven't been carried forward . . . I use my own individual system . . . No. No, not me, Mr Duxbury. Well, I'm sure you'll find that there's a very simple explanation . . . What? 810 Monday morning? Yes, of course I'll be there. Prompt. Thank you, Mr. Duxbury. Thank you for ringing. Good-bye, then . . . *(BILLY puts down the telephone for a moment and is lost in depression.*

DREAM *Fantasizing*

He brightens as, in his imagination *he addresses his employer.)* Well, look Duxbury – we're not going to argue over trivialities. As soon as I've finalised my arrangements with Mr. Boon I'll get in touch with you. *(He picks up the telephone.)* Hello, Duxbury? . . . I'm afraid the answer is 'no'. I fully agree that a partnership sounds very attractive – but 820 frankly my interests lie in other directions. I'm quite willing to invest in your business, but I just have not the time to take over the administrative side . . . Oh, I agree that you have a sound proposition there . . . Granted! I take your point, Mr Duxbury. What's that little saying of yours?

He is treating Mr D as nothing in his fantasy world

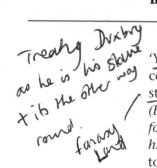

*Treating Duxbury
as he is his slave
+ its the other way
round.
fantasy land*

He has to

'You've got to come down to earth.' It's not a question of
coming down to earth, old man. Some of us belong in the
stars. The best of luck, Mr Duxbury, and keep writing . . .
*(BILLY breaks off as BARBARA approaches down the stairs and,
for her benefit, he goes off into another fantasy as she passes   830
him and enters the living-room.)* Well, doctor, if the leg's got
to come off – it's got to come off . . . *(BILLY replaces the
telephone and looks speculatively at the living-room door.)* It's
not a question of coming down to earth, Mr. Duxbury. *(He
pauses.)* Some of us, Mr Duxbury, belong in the stars. — *almost as if
he believes its
true.*

BILLY, *who has now regained his self-confidence, enters the
living-room and crosses towards BARBARA with her glass of
port.*

THE CURTAIN FALLS

the administrative side *'running the business'; 'making decisions'*

WRITING: In pairs, list the lies that Billy tells before page 30. Then
update the list, noting especially the lies he tells after promising not to
lie any more.

WRITING: Re-read Billy's speech from the moment he picks up the
telephone (page 34). Note down what you think his thoughts might be, as the
speech develops. E.g. line 802: Put on a posh voice; line 803 Oh no! It's Duxbury!
Quick! What's my excuse? . . .

ACT 2

*It is late afternoon the same day and just after tea-time in the
FISHER household. ALICE is moving in and out of the kitchen
clearing the tea-things from the living-room table. The best tea-
service has been brought out for BARBARA'S benefit, although
FLORENCE has insisted upon having her usual pint-pot. A
strange silence has fallen upon the living-room caused partly by
BARBARA'S disclosure that she has recently become engaged to
BILLY – and partly by FLORENCE'S insistence on taking her
time over her tea. FLORENCE, in fact, is the only one remaining
at the table. GEOFFREY has moved away to a chair and
BARBARA is seated on the couch. BILLY is in the hall engaged
in a phone conversation and has closed the door to the
living-room.*

BILLY
. . . Rita, will you listen for a minute! . . . No, listen to what   1
I'm telling you! The ring's still at the jeweller's! Of course
it's all right . . . Well, what's the sense in coming round
here now! It isn't here – I've just told you, it's at the
jeweller's . . . Rita! . . . *(He puts down the phone.)* Oh
blimey! . . . *(He takes up the phone and dials a number.)*

BARBARA
(In an attempt to break the silence.) Of course, we haven't
fixed the date or anything. *(There is a pause.)* We won't be
thinking of getting married for quite a while yet.

GEOFFREY
(A slight pause.) Well, what you going to live on? The pair of   10
you? He'll never have a bloody penny.

FLORENCE
And there was none of this hire purchase in them days.

hire purchase *This is a method of buying something and paying for it in
instalments.*

What you couldn't pay for you didn't have. I don't agree with it. He didn't either. It's only muck and rubbish when it's there.

ALICE returns from the kitchen and fills a tray with used tea-things. She picks up FLORENCE'S pint-pot.

I haven't finished with that yet. *(ALICE replaces the pot.)*

BILLY puts down the phone in exasperation. He picks it up and dials another number. ALICE returns to the kitchen with the tray.   **20**

Fantasy world as well

BARBARA   We had thought of a cottage in Devon.

GEOFFREY   Bloody Devon! He'll never get past the end of our street.

FLORENCE   She needn't have opened that tin of salmon – it's not been touched hardly.

BARBARA   I don't believe in long engagements – but I don't mind waiting.

GEOFFREY   You'll wait till bloody Domesday if you wait for that sackless article. He's not had a shave yet.

ALICE   *(Putting her head round the kitchen door.)* Come on, Mother!   **30**
It's only you we're waiting for.

FLORENCE   *(Mumbling to herself.)* She knows I haven't got to be rushed. I don't know what she does it for . . .

An awkward silence falls upon the living-room. BILLY speaks into the telephone.

BILLY   Arthur? . . . Look, you've got to do something for me. Stop Rita coming round here . . . Well, go round to their house! She's after the ring and Barbara's still got it . . . No, did she

---

? **Domesday** *Judgement Day; 'the end of the world'.*

sackless article *Geoffrey considers Billy to be lazy and lacking in drive.*

heckerslike! I told you they were aspirins. Don't stand there
yattering, get your skates on!   40

He slams down the receiver.

FLORENCE   *(Who has been mumbling quietly to herself throughout the above
now raises her voice to address the sideboard.)* It's every tea-
time alike. Rush, rush, rush. They've got no consideration.
She knows I'm not well.

BARBARA   *(Politely.)* Billy was saying you'd not been well.

GEOFFREY   Take no notice of what he says – he'll have you as bloody
daft as his-self. *(BILLY opens the door and enters the living-
room.)* You'll stand talking on that phone till you look like a
bloody telephone. Who was it, then?   50

BILLY   Only Arthur.

GEOFFREY   What's he bloody want?

BILLY   Oh – nothing.

GEOFFREY   He takes his time asking for it.

ALICE   *(Enters from the kitchen.)* How's his mother?

BILLY   *(Crossing to the fireplace.)* All right – considering.

BARBARA   Arthur's mother? Has she been ill?

GEOFFREY   That's the bloody tale he's come home with.

---

yattering *'chattering'*

DISCUSSION: As a class, discuss what seems to have happened
between the end of Act 1 and the beginning of Act 2.
   In particular, (a) list the things that Billy is worried about and what
   he might have tried to do in an attempt to sort out his problems; and
(b) discuss what kind of things have just been said in the conversation around the
tea table.

BILLY	*(Shuffling awkwardly in front of the fire.)* She's been off-colour, but she's all right.

60

GEOFFREY	By, if I don't knock some sense into you! Stand up straight and get your hands out of your pockets! You want to get married, you do!
FLORENCE	She wants to sew them up. With a needle and cotton. She should sew them up.
GEOFFREY	You'll have to brighten your ideas up, then!
FLORENCE	A needle and a bit of black cotton. That'd stop him. Then he couldn't put them in his pockets.
ALICE	Mother, haven't you finished that tea yet! Why don't you finish it by the fire. I've got to get cleared up.

70

FLORENCE	*(Rising and crossing slowly to sit by the fire.)* I can't be up and down – up and down – every five minutes. She knows it doesn't do me any good. And that fire's too hot. He banks it up till it's like a furnace in here. I can't be putting up with it.
ALICE	*(Clearing the remains off the table.)* Well, it's all very well, Mother, I like to get things done. Then it's finished with.
BARBARA	Can I be giving you a hand, Mrs Fisher?
ALICE	It's all right, Barbara. I don't know why our Billy doesn't wash up once in a while.

80

GEOFFREY	He can't wash his bloody self, never mind the pots.
BARBARA	*(Rising and crossing towards the kitchen.)* I don't mind.
	BARBARA and ALICE go off into the kitchen. BILLY crosses to sit on the couch and GEOFFREY rises. There is an embarrassed silence. There is a first attempt at contact between BILLY and his father.
GEOFFREY	She doesn't have much to say for herself . . . Where do you say she works then?

BILLY	Turnbull and Mason's.
GEOFFREY	Who?
BILLY	Solicitors. Up Sheepgate.
GEOFFREY	Oh aye?
BILLY	Shorthand-typist.
GEOFFREY	She likes her food, doesn't she? She'll take some keeping. By bloody hell! She had her share of that pork pie, didn't she?
BILLY	She lives up Cragside. On that new estate.
GEOFFREY	She'll need to live up Cragside the way she eats. She can shift them tinned oranges when she starts, can't she? Mind you, she needs it. She's a big lass, isn't she? Big-boned.
BILLY	Yes.
GEOFFREY	*(After a pause.)* You're reckoning on getting married then?
BILLY	Thinking about it.
GEOFFREY	You've got your bloody self engaged, anyroad.
BILLY	Yes.
GEOFFREY	So she was saying. You never told us.
BILLY	No. I was meaning to.
GEOFFREY	That was a bit of a daft trick to do, wasn't it?
BILLY	Oh, I don't know.
GEOFFREY	I mean, at your age like. You're only young yet. You're not old enough to start thinking about getting married.
BILLY	There's no hurry.
GEOFFREY	No. But you'll have to put your mind to it some time.
BILLY	Yes.
GEOFFREY	I mean, you can't go carrying-on the way you've been

90

100

110

carrying-on – now, you know. Messing about with different lasses.

BILLY   No – I know. I realise that.

GEOFFREY   You've not only yourself to consider. I don't see why you couldn't have waited a bit. I don't see why you couldn't have told us – your mother and me.   120

BILLY   I've said – I was meaning to.

GEOFFREY   She's not – you haven't got her into trouble – mean, there's nothing like that about it, is there?

BILLY   No . . . No – 'course not.

BILLY looks across at his father and we feel, for a moment, that they are about to make some point of contact.

GEOFFREY   Well, that's something, anyroad. I suppose she's all right. Just with you not saying anything, that's all.

BILLY   Yes.

GEOFFREY   Only you'll have to start thinking about getting married.   130
Saving up and that.

BILLY   There's plenty of time yet.

FLORENCE   Well, she didn't touch none of that salmon, I know that. Nobody did. She puts too much out. There's some folk would be glad of that. I tell her . . .

BILLY shows some impatience.

GEOFFREY   'Course, I don't believe in interfering. You've made your mind up. I don't want you to come to me and say that I stopped you doing it.

? **got her into trouble** *'got her pregnant'*

41

BILLY	Well, Dad, it's not that simple. I've not really decided what we'll be doing yet.	140
GEOFFREY	You couldn't do no worse than us when we started. Me and your mother. We'd nothing – I hadn't two ha'pennies to scratch my backside with. We had to manage.	
BILLY *Many*	I'm not bothered about managing, Dad. It's just that I hadn't made my mind up.	
GEOFFREY	*(Almost reverting back to his normal antagonism.)* Well, you want to get your bloody mind made up, lad. Right sharp. Before she does it for you.	
BILLY	You see . . .	150
FLORENCE	*(Interrupting.)* I told her. I had my say. I told her, you don't get married till you're twenty-one.	
BILLY	Just a minute, Grandma . . .	
FLORENCE *Florence interfering*	*(Ignoring him.)* You can do as you like then, I said. Only, I said, don't come running back to me when you can't manage. I said you'll have it to put up with	
BILLY	*(Completely exasperated.)* For Christ's sake belt up!	
GEOFFREY	*(Losing his temper completely.)* You what! *(He moves across and grabs BILLY by his shirt.)* You what did you say? What was that? What did you say?	160
BILLY	*(Frightened but unrepentant.)* I merely remarked . . .	
GEOFFREY *Denigrating his son*	*(Shouting.)* Talk bloody properly when you talk to me! You were talking different a minute ago, weren't you? What did you just say to your grandma? What did you just say?	
	ALICE enters from the kitchen.	

---

ha'pennies *'half-pennies'; old coins worth roughly a fifth of a modern penny.*

---

unpleasant domestic rows with Dad + claustrophobia of home r 2 reasons why billy lives in his fantasy world

ALICE	Hey, what's all this row? *(She indicates the kitchen.)* Don't you know we've got somebody here?
GEOFFREY	I can't help who's here! She might as well know what he is! Because I'll tell her! *(Shaking him.)* He's ignorant! That's what you are, isn't it? Ignorant! Ignorant! Ignorant! Isn't it? 170
ALICE	Well, don't pull him round. That shirt's clean on.
GEOFFREY	*(Releasing his hold on BILLY.)* I'll clean shirt him before I've finished!
ALICE	Well, what's he done?
GEOFFREY	I'll clean shirt him round his bloody ear-hole. With his bloody fountain pens and his bloody suede shoes! Well, he doesn't go out tonight. I know where he gets it from. He stops in tonight and tomorrow night as well.
BILLY	Look . . .
GEOFFREY	Don't 'look' me! With your look this and look that! And 180 you can get all that bloody books and rubbish or whatever it is cleared out of that sideboard cupboard as well! Before I chuck 'em out – and you with 'em!
BILLY	What's up? They're not hurting you are they?
	BARBARA enters and stands in the kitchen doorway uncertainly.
GEOFFREY	No, and they're not bloody hurting you either!
ALICE	*(Quietly.)* Well, I don't know what you've done now.
GEOFFREY	Answering back at his grandmother. If that's what they learned him at grammar school I'm glad I'm bloody uneducated! Anyroad, I've finished with him! He knows 190 where there's a suitcase. If he wants to go to London he can bloody well go.
ALICE	*(Sharply.)* Oh, but he's not.
GEOFFREY	I've finished with him. He can go.

ALICE   Oh, but he's not.

GEOFFREY   He's going! He can get his bloody things together! He's going out!

ALICE   Oh, but he's not. Oh, but he's not. Oh, but he is not!

BILLY   *(Trying to get a word in.)* Look, can I settle this . . .

GEOFFREY   *(Interrupting.)* It's ever since he started work. Complaining   200
about this and that and the other. If it isn't his boiled eggs
it's something else. You have to get special bloody
wheatflakes for him because there's a bloody plastic bloody
submarine in the packet. Splashing about in the kitchen at
his age. He wants putting away. Well, I've had enough – he
can go.

ALICE   Oh, but he's not. Now, you just listen to me, Geoffrey. He's
not old enough to go to London or anywhere else.

GEOFFREY   He's old enough to get himself engaged. He thinks he is.
He's old enough and bloody daft enough.   210

ALICE   Well, you said yourself. He doesn't think. He gets ideas in
his head.

GEOFFREY   He can go. I've finished with him.

ALICE   Oh, but he is not. Not while I'm here.

BARBARA   *(Who has been staring at FLORENCE.)* Mrs Fisher . . .

GEOFFREY   *(Ignoring her.)* He wants to get into the bloody army, that's
what he wants to do.

ALICE   *(Spiritedly.)* Yes, and you want to get into that bloody army
as well.

BARBARA   Mrs Fisher. I don't think Billy's grandma's very well.   220

He wants putting away *'He ought to be in a mental institution.'*

Yes, and you want to get into the bloody army as well. *Is Alice
alluding to the fact that Geoffrey avoided fighting in the war?*

ALICE, GEOFFREY and BILLY turn and look at FLORENCE who's sitting slumped in her chair.

ALICE   *(Rushing across to her mother.)* Now look what you've done!

GEOFFREY   *(To BILLY.)* I hope you're bloody satisfied now. She's had another do.

ALICE   It's no use blaming him, Geoffrey. You're both as bad as each other. Well, don't just stand there – get me the smelling salts.

BARBARA   *(Coming forward.)* Can I be doing anything, Mrs Fisher?

WRITING: Draw a graph showing how Geoffrey comes closer to Billy here, but only for a while. On the y-axis, chart the closeness on a scale of 0 to 10. On the x-axis, write in the first words of each line of key moments in their conversation. Go from the middle of page 40 to the end of page 43 ('He can go.').

y

```
     10
 C    9
 L    8
 O    7
 S    6
 E    5
 N    4
 E    3
 S    2
 S    1
      0 _____ x
```

| You're reckoning on getting married then? | .... | .... | .... | .... |

HOT-SEATING: In groups of four, hot-seat Geoffrey. Ask him about his attempts to get closer to Billy and why they failed. Why, for example, does he object to Billy's fountain-pen and suede shoes?

ALICE	No . . . no, it's all right. She's getting old, that's all. He'll see **230** to it.
GEOFFREY	*(Crossing to the sideboard he searches through the drawers.)* It's happening too bloody often is this. We can't be having this game every fortnight – neither sense nor reason in it.
ALICE	Well, she can't help it, Geoffrey. It's not her fault.
GEOFFREY	She'll have to see that bloody doctor. If I've to take time off and take her myself – she'll have to see him.
ALICE	She won't see him.
GEOFFREY	It's getting past a joke is this. *(Rifling through a second drawer.)* I wish you'd keep them salts in the same place. **240** Never here when you want them.
ALICE	*(Patting her mother's wrists.)* Hurry up, Geoffrey!
FLORENCE	*(Who has been slowly coming round during the above begins to mumble.)* I told her about that fire. Banking it up. I get too hot and then I go off. They don't think. Rushing me with my tea.
ALICE	It's all right, Mother. You'll be all right.
GEOFFREY	*(He locates the bottle of smelling salts and crosses and hands them to ALICE.)* Does she want these bloody salts or not?
ALICE	*(Taking the bottle from GEOFFREY.)* She'd better have them. **250**
	(She opens the bottle and holds it under FLORENCE'S nose.)
FLORENCE	Feathers.
GEOFFREY	She's off. She's bloody rambling.
FLORENCE	She wants to burn some feathers. Never mind salts. I can't

smelling salts *These are crystals, in a small bottle, used to revive someone who is feeling faint.*

	be doing with salts. They make me bilious.	
ALICE	It's all right, Mother. *(To GEOFFREY.)* We'd better get her upstairs. She's too hot here anyway.	
GEOFFREY	She'll be too bloody cold if she doesn't see that doctor. It's not fair on us. It's us that has it to put up with.	
BARBARA	Shall I fetch you a glass of water?	260
ALICE	No – she doesn't have water. She'll be all right in a minute.	
GEOFFREY	It's happening too regular is this. It's every week alike. And it's always on bloody Saturdays. We can't even sit down to us tea in peace.	
ALICE	Don't go on at her – you'll only make her worse. Just help me get her off to bed.	
GEOFFREY	*(Putting his arm round FLORENCE and raising her to her feet. He is gruffly compassionate.)* Come on then, Mother. Let's be having you. She's a bloody ton weight. She puts some weight on for somebody who never eats nothing. *(To FLORENCE.)* You're putting weight on.	270
ALICE	Don't stand there, Billy. Help your father.	
GEOFFREY	*(Piloting FLORENCE towards the door.)* By bloody hell – don't ask him to do nothing. He'll drop her down the bedroom stairs.	
ALICE	*(Crossing to help him.)* You never give him a chance.	
	ALICE and GEOFFREY support FLORENCE and move off through the hall and up the stairs.	

make me bilious *'upset my stomach'*

She'll be too bloody cold . . . *One of Geoffrey's few jokes!*

to sit down to us tea *Geoffrey's Yorkshire dialect ('us tea') is stronger than Billy's.*

FLORENCE   They ought to put a bed down here . . . Them stairs is too steep . . . They could have got the bungalow . . .   **280**

GEOFFREY   Now steady . . . Steady on, lass . . . Plenty of time.

FLORENCE continues to mumble to herself as they go upstairs. We cannot hear what she is saying but one sentence comes out plainly as they disappear into the bedroom.

FLORENCE   It's all these blacks . . .

In the living-room there is an embarrassed silence between BILLY and BARBARA. BILLY absent-mindedly picks up FLORENCE'S handbag and looks inside it. He goes through the contents idly and takes out an obsolete ration book.

BILLY   Do you know, she still keeps her old ration book?   **290**

BARBARA   I noticed she didn't look very well. Even at tea-time. I noticed but I didn't like to say anything.

BILLY   *(After a pause.)* You wouldn't think she'd been all over the world, would you? Paris – Cairo – Vienna.

BARBARA   *(Incredulously.)* Who? Your grandma?

BILLY   My grandad was in the Diplomatic Corps. Before he had his leg off. He could speak seven languages, you know. They went all over.

Lying

BARBARA   *(Completely disbelieving him she decides to ignore this statement.)* Do you think your mother's going to like me, pet?   **300**

BILLY   He was in the French Foreign Legion for nine years.

?   **ration book** *During World War II, food and many other commodities were in short supply. Everybody had a ration book that was stamped to show they had received their meat ration, for example, for the week.*

Incredulously *'not believing him'*

Diplomatic Corps *A very 'posh' part of the Civil Service, working abroad.*

BARBARA	I think we should get on with each other. It's better when you do – really. When families stick together. Why didn't you tell them we'd got engaged?
BILLY	I was going to. Did you show them the ring?
BARBARA	*(Examining the ring.)* Of course. I show it to everybody. It's lovely. I won't be completely happy until I've got the other one to go with it.
BILLY	Darling . . . *(Taking her hand.)* You will always love me, won't you?
BARBARA	You know I will.
BILLY	*(His fingers on the engagement ring.)* I still say this ring's too big. Why won't you let me get it altered?
BARBARA	*(Pulling her hand away.)* I don't think it's too big. Anyway, I want everybody to see it first. — conventional.
BILLY	Well, don't blame me if you lose it. My mother was saying it was nearly coming off while you were washing up. It'll only take a couple of days. And then it'll be there for ever. *(Romantically.)* For ever and ever . . .
BARBARA	Sweet . . .
BILLY	So go on, then. Give me it. You can have it back on Wednesday.
BARBARA	No, I'll never take it off. Never – never.
BILLY	Give me the cowing ring!
BARBARA	Billy!
BILLY	*(Moving away from her in disgust.)* Oh, please yourself, then.

310

320

French Foreign Legion *Volunteer section of the French army based mainly in north Africa – famous for the toughness of its soldiers.*

Don't say I didn't warn you.

RITA approaches the house through the garden. She is a small girl with blonde hair – seventeen years old but she dresses to look much older. She is common and hard and works in a snack bar.   330

BARBARA   Now you're cross. Don't be, pet. I'll take care of it. And I'll never lose it.

RITA rings the bell.

BILLY   Just a minute.

He crosses into the hall and opens the front door.

Rita!

RITA   *(Moving forward menacingly.)* Right, I suppose you . . .

BILLY   *(Interrupting her.)* Just a minute!

Slapstick with doors.

He slams the door on RITA and moves across the hall to speak to   340
BARBARA.

Just a minute! *(He closes the living-room door.)*

ALICE   *(Appearing at the top of the staircase.)* Who is it, Billy?

BILLY   Just a minute!

BILLY opens the front door and enters the garden, closing the door behind him.

BARBARA takes <u>an orange from her handbag</u> and is peeling it as the lights fade down on the living-room and the lights come up on the garden set.

BR

Hallo, Rita.   350

RITA   *(Her conversation consists mainly of clichés and expressions*

---

common *'vulgar and coarse'*

clichés *over-used, 'stale' expressions*

picked up on amorous evenings spent with friendly American airmen.) Ooh! Look what's crawled out of the cheese!

BILLY   Hallo, Rita – sorry I can't ask you in.

RITA   Get back in the knife-box, big-head.

BILLY   We're flooded. The pipes have burst.   *immediate lie*

RITA   Are you kidding? Here, pull the other one – it's got bells on it.

BILLY   *Sees through the lies*
                 What's the matter, darling? Is anything wrong?

RITA   Hark at Lord Muck. Don't come the innocent with me. You   360
                 know what's wrong. I thought you were going to your
                 uncle's on Wednesday night.

BILLY   I did go to my uncle's. My Uncle Herbert's. *(Jewish)*

RITA   Well, you didn't then – because somebody saw you. Sitting
                 in the Gaumont. With your arm round a lass eating
                 oranges.

BILLY   They didn't see me. I was at my Uncle Ernest's playing
                 Monopoly.

RITA   *(Imitating him.)* At my Uncle Ernest's playing Monopoly.
                 You rotten liar! You're just muck. You're rotten, that's what   370
                 you are. And where's my engagement ring?

BILLY   I'm glad you asked me that question. Because I called into
                 the shop this morning and the man said it might be
                 another week.   *lie*

RITA   *(Again imitating him.)* The man said it might be another
                 week. You're worse than muck. You're rotten.

---

 amorous evenings spent with friendly American airmen *There were many US airmen stationed in Britain after the war. Rita has clearly 'been around' with them.*

BILLY	No, because they can't do it up here. They've got to send it to Bradford. They've got three people off ill.
RITA	*(Again imitating him.)* Three people off ill. Yes, I suppose they're all having their legs off. To hear you talk everybody's having their leg off. And another thing, I thought I was coming round for my tea this afternoon. To meet your rotten mother. 380
BILLY	Yes, darling, but something happened. My grandma was taken ill. Last Thursday. They've got her in bed.
RITA	Well, I am going to see your rotten mother – I'll tell you that. My name's not 'Silly', you know. Either you get me that rotten ring back or I'm going to see your rotten mother.
BILLY	*(Attempting to quieten her.)* Ssh, darling! 390
RITA	*(Raising her voice.)* And your rotten father! And your rotten grandmother!

In a wild attempt to quieten RITA, BILLY takes her in his arms and kisses her. She responds with an automatic animal passion. They break away.

	You are rotten to me, Billy. I'm not kidding, you know. I still want that ring back. *(Her voice rises again.)* And my dad wants to know where it is as well. We're supposed to be engaged, you know.
BILLY	You once said you didn't want to marry me. 400
RITA	Don't come that tale with me. I said I didn't want to live in a rotten cottage in Devon – that's all.
BILLY	We'll live wherever you like, darling. Nothing matters as

She responds with automatic animal passion. *Rita mechanically 'switches on' a passionate physical response.*

Cliche

long as we're together.

RITA	Well, can you get it back tonight then?
BILLY	Of course I can, darling. If that's what you want. *(He kisses her again.)* Darling, darling, darling.
RITA	*(Pushing BILLY away as his hand creeps round her back.)* Hey, Bolton Wanderer! Keep your mucky hands to yourself.
BILLY	Tell me you're not cross with me, darling.
RITA	*(Imitating him.)* Tell me you're not cross . : . Put another record on, we've heard that one. And get that ring back.
BILLY	I will. I promise, darling. I'll go down to the shop. I'll give it to you tonight – at the dance.
RITA	You'd better do – or else there'll be bother. I wouldn't like to be in your shoes if my father comes round. And he will, you know. And he won't stand arguing in the garden. *(BILLY kisses her again.)* Go on, then. Go in and get your coat on – and get off for that ring.
BILLY	See you tonight, darling.
RITA	Never mind see you tonight, shops'll be shut in half an hour. You'll get off now. Go on, then, get your coat. You can walk me down as far as the bus-stop. Go on, Dateless, don't stand there catching flies.
BILLY	I can't go yet.
RITA	Why not? What's stopping you?
BILLY	I'm waiting to go to the lavatory. My mam's on.
RITA	I'll be walking on. You catch me up.

410

420

Bolton Wanderer *Another cliché: Rita refers to the football team and Billy's 'wandering' hands.*

RITA walks off, slowly, down the garden and goes. BILLY enters the house. As he crosses through the hall the lights fade in the garden and come up in the living-room. BARBARA is just finishing eating the orange.   **430**

BILLY   Hey, listen! I've just had my fortune told by a gipsy.

BARBARA   I've eaten a whole orange while I've been waiting.

BILLY   She says there's a curse on me.

BARBARA   Your mother's not come down yet. Neither has your father.

BILLY   I'm going to experience sorrow and misfortune but after a long journey things will start to go right. Hey, she had a baby on her back like a Red Indian.

BARBARA   Do you think she'll be all right – your grandmother?   **440**

BILLY crosses and sits in the armchair.

BILLY   Who? Oh, my grandma! Yes, she'll be all right. It's just that she's got this rare disease – they're trying a new drug out on her.

BARBARA   She looked as though she was having some kind of fit at first. I noticed when you were having that row with your father.

BILLY   They've only tried it out three times – this drug. Once on President Eisenhower, then the Duke of Windsor and then my grandma.   **450**

[handwritten: Can't Disguise between Different sorts of fantasy. Devon etc.]

[handwritten: ~ See through that]

BARBARA   Honestly! No wonder your father gets cross with you.

BILLY   How do you mean?

BARBARA   Well, all these stories you keep telling – no wonder he keeps losing his temper.

President Eisenhower, the Duke of Windsor *Billy picks two of the most famous world figures of the time: the US President and the former King.*

BILLY	Oh, you don't take any notice of him.
BARBARA	Billy?
BILLY	What?
BARBARA	What was your father saying? About you going to London?
BILLY	Did he? When? I never heard him.
BARBARA	When he was talking about answering back at your grandmother. When he got hold of your shirt. He said, 'If you want to go to London you can "B" well go'. He swore. 460
BILLY	I know. He's been summonsed twice for using bad language.
BARBARA	Yes, but what did he mean?
BILLY	What? About going to London?
BARBARA	Yes.
BILLY	Ah, well – there's a very interesting story behind that.
BARBARA	No, Billy, this is important – to us. You've got to think about me now.
BILLY	*(He rises and crosses towards her.)* It's for you I'm doing it, my darling. 470

He could make up if he chose to

 summonsed *'taken to court'*

DISCUSSION: As a class, discuss what you think Florence's role is in this play. What part does she play in the story? Predict what you think is going to happen to her.

ACTING: In groups of three, act out the scene from the top of page 49 ('. . . we'd got engaged?') to the end of page 50 ('Hello Rita.'). Try to convey Billy's desperate attempts to get the ring and his panic when Rita arrives.

WRITING: Look closely at Rita's language and, in particular, note down the clichés that she uses. Discuss your notes with a neighbour.

BARBARA	What do you mean?
BILLY	*(Sitting down beside her and taking her hand he goes off into a fantasy.)* Isn't it obvious? How can we go on living like this?
BARBARA	*(Automatically freeing her hand she takes an orange from her handbag.)* What do you mean, pet? Like what?
BILLY	In this – this atmosphere. Do you honestly think that we could ever be happy – I mean really happy – here?
BARBARA	Where?
BILLY	In this house. There's the shadow of my father across this house. He's a bitter man, Barbara. 480
BARBARA	*(She settles down and begins to peel the orange.)* Why? What for? What about?
BILLY	He's jealous. Every time he looks at me he sees his own hopes and the failure of his own ambitions.
BARBARA	Your father?
BILLY	He had his dreams once. He can't bear it – seeing me on the brink of success. He was going to be a writer too.— Lie ↳ Fantasy
BARBARA	Billy, if this is going to be another of your stories . . .
BILLY	You don't have to believe me. The evidence is here – in this house. 490
BARBARA	Evidence? How do you mean – evidence?
BILLY	*(Pointing to the sideboard.)* It's all in there.
BARBARA	What is?
BILLY	Go and look for yourself. In that cupboard.

> **How can we go on living like this?** *Billy sees himself playing a part in a romantic film.*

Mr Ishmm

56 *

BARBARA rises and crosses to the sideboard. She tugs at the handle on BILLY'S cupboard.

writing/performing TV
failure of DAD

BARBARA   It's locked.

BILLY   (*Meaningly.*) Yes.

BARBARA   Where's the key?   500

overdramatic

BILLY   God knows. I was four years old when that was locked, Barbara. It's never been opened since.

BARBARA   (*Crossing towards BILLY.*) Well, what's supposed to be in it?

BILLY   Hopes! Dreams! Ambitions! The life work of a disillusioned man. Barbara, there must be forty or fifty unpublished novels in that cupboard. All on the same bitter theme.

BARBARA   (*In half-belief.*) Well, we can't all be geniuses.

BILLY   Perhaps not. But he crucified himself in the attempt. Sitting night after night at that table. Chewing at his pen. And when the words wouldn't come he'd take it out on us.   510

crap

BARBARA   But what about going to London? What about our cottage in Devon?

ALICE emerges from the bedroom and comes down the stairs.

BILLY   Well, it's all down south, Barbara. We could live in the New

MORE
Boochhg

Forest. We could have a cottage there – a woodman's cottage – in a clearing.

BARBARA   I think I'd be frightened. Living in a forest.

REALLY BELIEVES IT

BILLY   (*He puts his arm round her.*) Not with me to look after you, you wouldn't.

BILLY rises awkwardly as ALICE enters the room. ALICE is   520
faintly preoccupied. She crosses towards the kitchen and speaks almost to herself.

ALICE   Well, she seems to be resting.

ALICE goes into the kitchen. There is a slight feeling of

embarrassment between BILLY and BARBARA and then BARBARA speaks to break the silence.

BARBARA	Are we going out dancing tonight?
BILLY	If you like . . . *(He claps his hand to his forehead in an over-dramatic gesture.)* Oh, no! Just remembered!
BARBARA	*(Suspiciously.)* What?
BILLY	I promised to go round to my Uncle Herbert's tonight. To play Monopoly. It's his birthday.
BARBARA	Funny you never told me before. You're always having to go round to your Uncle Herbert's. Anyway, I thought it was your Uncle Ernest who played Monopoly?
BILLY	Ah, well . . . I'm glad you asked me that question. You see, my Uncle Herbert . . .
BARBARA	*(Interrupting),* Oh, don't bother. You and your relatives. If I didn't know you better I'd think you had another girl.
BILLY	Darling! What a thing to say!
BARBARA	You know that Liz is back in town, don't you?
BILLY	Liz who?
BARBARA	You know who. That dirty girl. I'm surprised you weren't ashamed to be seen with her.
BILLY	Oh, her . . . I haven't seen her for donkeys years.

ALICE enters from the kitchen. She is carrying a tumbler containing a white liquid which she is stirring with a spoon.

ALICE	Her breathing's all right – she's still awake, though. I think she'd be better if we could get her off to sleep.
BARBARA	She was looking tired this afternoon.
ALICE	*(Gently reprimanding.)* Well, I blame you as much as anybody. You set your father off and then it sets her off. I've told you time and time again.

530

540

550

(handwritten: ironic)

58

BILLY	*(Half-ashamed.)* She's all right now, is she, then?
ALICE	Is she ever all right?
BARBARA	Are you quite sure there's nothing I can do? Could she eat an orange?
ALICE	I'm going to get the doctor in to her – be on the safe side. Whether she wants him or not. Your father's sitting with her. *(She hands BILLY the tumbler.)* Can you take this up without spilling it?

           560

BILLY	*(Taking the tumbler reluctantly.)* Who? Me?
ALICE	Either that or ring the doctor up for me. *(Rather impatiently.)* But do something, lad, don't just stand there.

ALICE turns away from him and walks briskly into the hall where she picks up the phone. BILLY stands indecisively for a moment and then crosses through into the hall and up the stairs as ALICE dials the number. She waits for a reply and glances up at BILLY who has, for no reason at all, developed a limp. She calls up to him.

           570

Now, what are you playing at!

BILLY stops limping and quickens his pace and goes into the bedroom as ALICE turns back to the phone.

Hello, is that the surgery? . . . Well, it's Mrs Fisher, forty-two Park Drive . . . Yes, that's right. Only it's my mother again. Mrs Boothroyd. Do you think the doctor could call round? . . . Oh, dear. Only we've got her in bed again . . . I've given her her tablets – and the mixture . . . Well, will you ask him to come round as soon as he can? . . . Yes, yes, I will, I will – thank you very much. Good-bye.

           580

ALICE replaces the phone and crosses into the living-room.

You don't like to bother them on a Saturday but what else can you do?

BARBARA	Is the doctor coming, Mrs Fisher?

ALICE	He's coming sometime – when he's ready. It'll be nine o'clock again, I suppose. He's already out on his calls.
BARBARA	I shouldn't worry. He'll be round as soon as he can.
ALICE	*(Sitting.)* You can't help worrying sometimes. If I don't worry nobody else will. It's just getting me down, is this. It's just one thing after another. **590**
BARBARA	*(Returns to her seat on the couch and takes up the orange.)* Would you like a piece of orange, Mrs Fisher?
ALICE	*(She looks up and, for the first time, realises that BARBARA is trying to help.)* No. No, thank you. Not just at this minute, love. Thank you.
BARBARA	Would it be better if I went? *(Half-rising.)* I mean if I'm in the way.
ALICE	No, don't be silly. You sit yourself down. I'm only sorry it's happened while you were here.
BARBARA	*(Returning to her seat.)* You can't arrange illness, can you? **600**
ALICE	You can't. I only wish you could. Only she has these turns and all you can do is put her to bed. But she always seems to pick the most awkward times. Still, you can't blame her. It's not her fault. You might think it is to hear him talk. You'd think she does it on purpose, to listen to him.
BARBARA	She might be better before the doctor comes.
ALICE	It wears me out, I know that. And if it isn't her it's our Billy. I don't know what we're going to do with him.
BARBARA	I think he wants to help – but he doesn't like to offer.
ALICE	He didn't use to be like this. He's got to grow up sometime. **610** I don't know, it might be better if he did go to London. It might put some sense into him if he had to look after himself.
BARBARA	Well, that's what I don't understand, Mrs Fisher. Is he going

to London?

ALICE	Well, he reckons he is. Hasn't he said anything to you?
BARBARA	Well, not really. I only heard what his father said. I tried to ask him.
ALICE	What did he say to you?
BARBARA	Nothing, really. *(She indicates the sideboard.)* He just started talking about that cupboard.
ALICE	Oh, don't talk to me about that cupboard. I don't know what he keeps in there. I'm frightened to ask, to tell you the honest truth.
BARBARA	He said it had been locked since he was four years old.
ALICE	I don't know why he says these things. I mean, what good does it do him? It's not as if he gets anything out of it.
BARBARA	I'm quite sure I don't know. He told me Mr Fisher was a captain on a petrol ship.
ALICE	Don't let his father hear you say that – else there'll be trouble. He'll murder him one of these days. If he knew all I know he'd have murdered him long ago. I could do it myself sometimes. And he says things we can find out about, that's what I don't understand. He told me that young lad who works in the fruit shop had gassed himself – and he knows I go in there every Tuesday.
BARBARA	I know. He says all kinds of things.
ALICE	I don't know where he'll end up – it's not our fault, I do know that. We've done our best for him. His father says it's since he started work – but I know different. It's ever since he went to that grammar school. He wanted to go, so we let him – he'd not been there five minutes before he wanted to leave. And we had it all to pay for, you know – he never appreciated it. School uniform, he loses his cap first week. Cricketing trousers, he never wore them. We bought him a

620

630

640

satchel and he let a lad run away with it. Then there was his books to pay for – well, he never reads them. It's just been a waste of time and money. You'd think he'd been dragged up. He's not cleaned his shoes for six months.

BARBARA   I tell him about his shoes. He takes no notice. And his hair   650
– he won't have a haircut, will he?

ALICE   Well, he doesn't take after me – or his father. And it's us that's got to clean up after him. He got them suede shoes so he wouldn't have to bother cleaning them – but you can't just not touch them. He trod in some dog-dirt on Tuesday and – do you know? – he walked it round this house for three days. I had to get a knife and scrape it off myself, in the finish. *(Distastefully, recalling the incident.)* Pooh! You could smell it all over the house. — UGLY D UGLY

BARBARA   My mother won't have a dog. And she hates cats.   660

ALICE   You can't keep on telling him – it just goes in one ear and out the other. He wants watching all the time, that's his trouble. You see, if he'd gone into the business with his father, like we wanted him to, we could have kept an eye on him more. But he won't listen. He went after all kinds of daft jobs. That lady in the Juvenile Employment Bureau, she lost patience with him. He wouldn't have this and he wouldn't have that. And she offered him some lovely jobs to begin with. He could have gone as a junior trainee at the Co-op Bank if he'd wanted to. She offered him that.   670

BARBARA   I know somebody who works there, she likes it. They've got their own social club.

ALICE   She just stopped bothering. She couldn't get any sense out of him. She asked him what he did want in the end and he

Juvenile Employment Bureau *A careers centre for young people.*

Sausages

told her he wanted to be either a merchant seaman or a concert pianist. Grammar school! You'd think he'd been to the Silly School. He shows me up.

BARBARA   How did he come to work for Shadrack and Duxbury's?

ALICE   Don't ask me. He'd been left school a fortnight and he was still no nearer a job – he wanted to work in the museum by   680 this time. We were sick and tired of having him lounging about the house. His father comes home one morning at twelve o'clock and finds him playing with some Plasticine. He went mad. He told him straight out. He says, you get out of this house, and get yourself a job, my lad, he says. And, he says, don't you dare come back without one – or I'll knock your blooming head right off your shoulders – only he didn't say blooming.

BARBARA   No, I can imagine.

ALICE   So, of course, our Billy goes out and waltzes back two hours   690 later and says he's working for an undertaker – start on Monday. He's been there ever since.

BARBARA   I don't think he likes it, though, does he?

ALICE   Like it or lump it, he's got to work for his living. Never mind going to London. He's got no mind of his own, that's his trouble. He listens to these pals he's got. What they do he's got to do. I'm only glad he's found himself a sensible lass, for once.

BILLY emerges from the bedroom and comes down the stairs.

BARBARA   I think it was that girl he used to go about with before he   700 met me, Mrs Fisher. That funny girl. That Liz. She used to put a lot of ideas into his head.

BILLY pauses at the foot of the stairs and listens to their conversation.

ALICE   Oh, that one. I've seen him with her. She looked as though a good bath wouldn't do her any harm. I don't know what kind of a family she comes from. I'm only glad she's gone.

BARBARA   She's come back again, didn't you know? She goes off all over, all the time. By herself. I don't think she's got any family. Do you know what I don't like about her, Mrs Fisher? She smokes and she keeps her cigarette in her mouth when she's talking. I could never do that. It looks common.   710

ALICE   You could always tell when he'd been out with her. The ideas he used to come home with. He comes home one night and says he wants to go off on holiday with her. To the Norfolk Broads, if you like. I told him – straight. I said, that's not the way we do things in this house. I said, if you want to go on holiday you can come to Morecambe with us – and if you don't you can stop at home.   720

BARBARA   I don't believe in mixed holidays – not before you're married.

ALICE   I'm sure you don't, love. You wouldn't be sitting here if you did, I can tell you.

BARBARA   He was saying you wouldn't mind if I went to Blackpool with him for a week – but I wouldn't. I don't believe in anything like that.

ALICE   He was saying what!

BILLY enters hastily and changes the subject.

BILLY   Hey, listen!   730

(ALICE and BARBARA turn to BILLY who is trying to think of something to say next. He tries in desperation to joke.)

Fifteen men under one umbrella and not one of them got wet.

(He evokes no reaction.)

It wasn't raining.

ALICE	*(To BARBARA.)* Well, you can't say you don't know what you're letting yourself in for. *(To BILLY.)* Stop acting so daft with people poorly. We've got enough on our plates without you.
BARBARA	How's your grandma, Billy? Is she any better?
ALICE	Has she gone off to sleep yet?
BILLY	She looks all right to me.
ALICE	Is your father all right with her? Would he like me to go up? Does he want anything?
BILLY	I don't know.
ALICE	No, and I don't suppose you care. *(Losing her temper.)* Have you had a wash since you got up this morning?
BILLY	'Course I have.

740

WRITING: In pairs look back at the conversation between Barbara and Billy (pages 54 – 58). Jot down what you think Barbara's thoughts are as the conversation progresses.

IMPROVISATION: In pairs, improvise a conversation between Billy and the careers advisor (see page 62).

STORYBOARDING: Billy Liar was made into a very successful film. Storyboard three frames of the scene (not in the film) in which Geoffrey returns to find Billy playing with Plasticene. The first frame might look like this:

Write notes on what the camera is doing (e.g. mid-shot of Geoffrey entyering the room; Billy's head in the frame).

Sketch what the viewer will see.

Write what the viewer will hear (e.g. sounds of Billy humming happily; Geoffrey saying 'What the . . . ?).

ALICE	Yes, a cat-lick. I bet you didn't take your shirt off, did you? You'll have to smarten your idea up, you know, if you want to go script-writing. They don't have them on the B.B.C. with mucky necks. You'll start washing your own shirts in future, I can't get them clean.

750

BILLY	*(Acutely embarrassed but, for BARBARA'S benefit, he pretends to be amused and winds an imaginary gramophone handle.)* Crikey Moses, she's off!
BARBARA	Well, you can't say you've had a shave this morning, Billy, because you haven't.
BILLY	I'm growing a beard, if you want to know.

760

ALICE	Oh no, you're not. We're having no beards in this house.
BARBARA	I don't think I'd like you with a beard, Billy.
ALICE	He's not having a beard.
BILLY	I'm having a bloody beard.
ALICE	Hey, hey, hey! Language! Don't you start coming out with that talk! Else you'll get a shock coming, big as you are! We get enough of that from your father.
BILLY	Well, I'm still having a beard. I can grow one in six weeks.
BARBARA	I don't think you should, Billy. Not if your mother doesn't want you to.

770

ALICE	He's got no say in the matter. If I say he doesn't grow a beard, he doesn't grow one.
BILLY	What's up with you? It's my stinking face!
ALICE	I'll not tell you again about that language! You can start to

cat-lick *'a very quick, skimpy wash'*

gramophone handle *Old-fashioned record-players needed winding up.*

Crikey Moses *This is a meaningless expression of mock despair.*

alter yourself, that's what you can do, my lad. We're not going on like this for much longer. Either brighten your ideas up or do as your father says – and get off to London or where you like. Because we're not going on like this, day in and day out! It's not fair on nobody!

BILLY	Oh, shut up!	780

ALICE And you can start watching what you say to people, as well. What did you say to me about that lad in the fruit shop? Gassing himself? And what have you been telling Barbara about that cupboard?

BILLY What cupboard?

ALICE You know very well what cupboard!

BILLY. I don't know what cupboard. How do you mean – cupboard?

BARBARA Your sideboard cupboard.

BILLY	What about it?	790

BARBARA That evidence you were talking about. In the cupboard. When you were four years old. All these unpublished novels. Where your father was chewing his pen up.

BILLY Oh, that! Oh, you should have said. No, you're getting mixed up. I was talking about his invoices that he writes out. He keeps them in that vase – I didn't say anything about any cupboard.

BARBARA (Shocked.) Billy Fisher! I don't know how you can stand there! He'll be struck down dead one of these days.

BILLY	(With a pretence at innocence.) What's up?	800

ALICE He can stand there as if butter wouldn't melt in his mouth.

BILLY I don't know what you're all on about.

BARBARA Oh yes, you do. Don't try and make it out as if it's me, Billy.

BILLY	It is you. Look – Barbara – you were sitting over there, weren't you? On that couch. Because you were eating an orange. And I was standing over there. Right? It is right, isn't it? You were sitting there and I was standing there.
BARBARA	Yes, but then you said your father . . .
ALICE	Never mind what he said, love, I know what he is.

RITA enters the garden and stands, for a moment, hesitantly outside the front door.   810

BILLY	Yes, you'll believe her, won't you?
ALICE	I'd believe anybody before you, Billy. I'm very sorry, but there it is. I'd believe Hitler before I'd believe you.
BILLY	Why don't you come straight out and call me a liar then!
ALICE	Well, you are one. I don't care who knows it.
BILLY	Well, that's a nice thing for a mother to say, isn't it?
ALICE	Yes, and you're a nice son for a mother to have, aren't you? You don't think what you're doing to me, do you? You never consider anybody except yourself. 820
BILLY	I suppose you do, don't you?
ALICE	Yes, I do. I worry about you, I know that.
BILLY	Well, what about me? Don't you think I worry? I worry about the H-bomb. You didn't know I nearly went on the Aldermaston march last Easter, did you? I don't want

I'd believe Hitler before I'd believe you. *This is a strong statement, given that Hitler, Nazi leader in World War II, was one of the most evil people of the 20th Century.*

the H-bomb . . . the Aldermaston march . . . *The first hydrogen bomb was exploded in 1952. From 1958 to 1963 there were protest marches against nuclear weapons on Aldermaston – an atomic research establishment in Berkshire.*

another war, you know. And what about all them refugees?
You never stop to consider them, do you? Or South Africa.

*At this point RITA makes up her mind and, without knocking,
marches into the house and into the living-room.*

Do you know, Barbara, if you were a blackie and we lived in   **830**
South Africa I'd be in gaol by now? Doing fifteen years.

(At which point he breaks off as RITA makes her entrance.)

Hallo, Rita.

RITA   *(To BILLY, indicating ALICE.)* It takes her some time to come
out of the lavatory, doesn't it? What's she been doing?
Writing her will out?

ALICE   *(Outraged.)* Do you usually come into people's houses
without knocking?

RITA   I do when people have got my private property. *(To BILLY.)*
Come on – give.   **840**

BILLY   Rita, I don't think you've ever met my mother, have you?

RITA   No, but she'll know me again, won't she? Come on, you
and your stinking rotten jewellers. I'm not daft, you know.

ALICE   *(Shocked.)* We're not having this! Where does she think
she is?

BILLY   *(Attempting to guide RITA towards the door he takes her elbow.)*
I'll just take Rita as far as the bus stop, mother.

RITA   *(Shrugging him away.)* Take your mucky hands off me, you
rotten toffee-nosed get. You didn't think I'd come in, did
you?   **850**

refugees *'people fleeing from their country due to war or oppression'*

. . . if you were black and lived in South Africa . . . *Under apartheid,
blacks and whites were not allowed to marry or have sexual relations.*

toffee-nosed *'stuck-up'; she thinks that Billy regards himself as superior.*

ALICE   No, but I think you'll go out, young lady. And if you've anything to say to my son you'd better just remember where you are.

BILLY   Well, I'm very glad you have come, Rita, because I feel I owe you a word of explanation.

RITA   *(Imitating him.)* Oooh, I feel I owe you a word of explanation. Get back in the cheese, with the other maggots.

ALICE   I'm not putting up with this – I shall bring his father down.

RITA   You can bring his rotten father down. I hope you do. And his rotten grandma.   **860**

BARBARA   Billy's grandma, for your information, happens to be ill in bed.

RITA   *(Turning to BARBARA for the first time.)* Oooh, look what the cat's brought in. Get Madam Fancy-knickers. I suppose this is your rotten sister. I thought she was supposed to be in a rotten iron lung.

BARBARA   For your information, I happen to be Billy's fiancée.

RITA   *(Imitating BARBARA.)* Oooh, for your information. Well for your information, he happens to be engaged to me. In front of a witness.   **870**

BILLY   How do you mean? What's witnesses got to do with it?

BARBARA   Billy, will you kindly tell me who this girl is?

RITA   *(Imitating her.)* Oooh, Billy, will you kindly tell me? Aw, go take a long walk on a short pier, you squint-eyed sow, you're nothing else.

---

iron lung *'a respirator'; a machine to help people to breathe.*

in front of a witness *In the 1950s a person could be taken to court for breaking off an engagement and charged with 'breach of promise'. (See 'I can go down to the Town Hall' on page 71.)*

ALICE	Barbara, would you kindly go upstairs and ask Mr. Fisher to come down for a minute?
RITA	You can fetch him down. Fetch all the rotten lot down. You can fetch the cowing iron lung down as well, for all I care. 880
ALICE	I've never been spoken to like this in all my days.
BARBARA	Shall I go up, Mrs. Fisher?
RITA	(*Imitating her.*) Oooh, shall I go up, Mrs. Fisher? If you can get up the stairs with them bow legs, you can.
ALICE	It's all right, Barbara. I'll deal with this young madam. I've met her type before.
BILLY	I think I can explain all this.
BARBARA	Yes, I think you've got some explaining to do, Billy.
RITA	He can explain until he's blue in the rotten face. It makes no difference to me. 890
ALICE	If I knew your mother, young lady, wouldn't I have something to say to her.
RITA	You can keep out of this. It's between me and him. (*To BILLY.*) Where's my ring? Has she got it? (*BARBARA'S right hand instinctively goes to her left.*) She has, hasn't she? You've given it to her, haven't you?
BILLY	Ah, well – yes, but you see . . . Only there's been a bit of a mix-up. You see, I thought Barbara had broken the engagement off.
BARBARA	Billy! 900
RITA	Yeh, well you've got another think coming if you think I'm as daft as she is. You gave that ring to me. And don't think you can go crawling out of it, 'cause you can't. You seem to forget I've got a witness, you know. I've got two. 'Cause Shirley Mitchem saw you giving me it, as well – so you needn't think she didn't. I can go down to the Town Hall, you know.

ALICE	Now, don't you come running in here with them tales, my girl. You know as well as I do he's under-age.
RITA	Ask him if he was under-age down at Foley Bottoms last night. 'Cause I'm not carrying the can back for nobody. He wasn't under-age then. He was over-age more like.
ALICE	Get out! Get out of my house!
BARBARA	Have you been untrue to me, Billy? I've got to know.
RITA	*(Imitating her.)* Oooh, have you been untrue to me, Billy! Get out of your push-chair, babyface. *(To BILLY.)* You're just rotten, aren't you? You are – you're rotten, all through. I've met some people in my time, but of all the lying, scheming . . . anyway, you gave that ring to me.
BILLY	Yes, but, look, Rita . . .
RITA	*(Interrupting.)* Don't talk to me, you rotten get. Well, she can have you – if she knows what to do with you, which I very much doubt. You rotten lying get. Garr – you think you're somebody, don't you? But you're nobody. You miserable lying rotten stinking get.
BILLY	Does this mean you're breaking off our engagement?
RITA	You don't get out of it like that. I want that ring.
BARBARA	*(Finding the right words at last.)* Billy, have you been – having relations with this girl?
RITA	*(Swinging round on BARBARA.)* What do you think he's been doing? Knitting a pullover? You know what you can do, don't you. You can give me that ring. Because it's mine.
ALICE	If you don't stop it this minute! *(To BILLY.)* As for you, I hope you know what you've done, because I don't.

Line numbers: 910, 920, 930

(handwritten annotation: *Reasons for failures*)

carrying the can back *'taking all the responsibility' (in the event of her being pregnant).*

having relations *Barbara cannot bring herself to make any reference to sex.*

RITA	Are you going to give me that ring?
BARBARA	I shall give the ring back to Billy – if and when I break off the engagement.
BILLY	*(Moving towards her.)* Barbara.
RITA	Yes, you can go to her. She can have you. And she knows what she can do, the squint-eyed, bow-legged, spotty, snotty-nosed streak of nothing.
BARBARA	And you know what you can do as well. You can wash your mouth out with soap and water.
RITA	*(Imitating.)* Oooh, you can wash your mouth out with soap and water. You could do with some soap in your ears, you've got carrots growing out of them. Well, you can give me that ring. Before I come over there and get it.
ALICE	You can get out of this house. I won't tell you again.
RITA	Save your breath for blowing out candles. I want my ring. *(Crossing towards BARBARA.)* Yes, and I'm going to get it.
ALICE	Get out of my house! Get out! Get out!
	GEOFFREY FISHER emerges from the bedroom and comes slowly down the stairs.
RITA	*(Moving right up to BARBARA.)* Are you going to give me that ring, or aren't you?
GEOFFREY	*(Half-way down the stairs.)* Mother! . . . Mother!

940

950

DISCUSSION: 'He's not having a beard.' As a class, discuss what restrictions are imposed upon Billy in the household. How differently are most 19-year-olds treated today?

DISCUSSION: As a class, discuss what Billy's speech beginning 'Well, what about me . . . ?' (page 68) reveals about him.

DISCUSSION: In pairs, discuss what Alice means by 'I've met her type before.' What is Rita's 'type.'? What is your own view of Rita?

RITA	Because you'll be in Emergency Ward Ten if I don't get it – right sharpish.
BARBARA	Don't you threaten me.
RITA	I won't threaten you – I'll flatten you! Give me that cowing ring back! *(She makes a grab for BARBARA'S hand.)* 960
BARBARA	*(Pushing her away.)* I won't . . . I won't . . .
ALICE	Will you stop it, the pair of you!
	GEOFFREY enters the room and stands in the doorway. He appears not to comprehend what is happening.
GEOFFREY	Mother!
	GEOFFREY'S word silences ALICE, BILLY and BARBARA who turn and look at him.
RITA	*(Unconcerned.)* Give me the ring!
GEOFFREY	You'd better come upstairs. Come now, I think she's dead. 970

THE CURTAIN FALLS   Florence is Dead

Emergency Ward Ten *A popular television soap at that time.*

FREEZE-FRAMING: In groups of five, create a 'waxworks tableau' or 'freeze-frame' to represent the moment when Geoffrey enters the room at the end of Act 2.

ACT 3

Invasion of Billys Space.

It is about half-past nine the same evening and quite dark in the garden outside the FISHERS' house. When the action of the play takes place in the garden, however, a street lamp comes up from the road beyond the garden and off-stage. There is also a small light in the porch of the house. As the curtain rises GEOFFREY FISHER is going through the contents of BILLY'S cupboard which are, at the moment, spread across the floor of the living-room by the sideboard. ALICE FISHER is sitting on a chair by the fire. She is obviously distraught by the death of her mother. GEOFFREY rummages through the envelopes and papers and then rises, shaking his head.

GEOFFREY	Well, I can't bloody find it. It's not here, anyway. He hasn't got it. It's about the only bloody thing he hasn't got.	1
ALICE	She might not have had one, Geoffrey – you know what she was like.	
GEOFFREY	*(Although he hasn't changed his vocabulary there is a more tender note than usual in his voice.)* Don't talk so bloody wet, lass. Everybody's got a birth certificate.	
ALICE	Well, you don't know, Geoffrey, they might not have had them in those days. She was getting on.	
GEOFFREY	Everybody's got a bloody birth certificate. They've had them since the year dot. If he's got it squat somewhere I'll bloody mark him for life.	10

repetitious

aggression

? got it squat *'got it hidden away'*

---

he does blame him for ever

ALICE	You can't blame our Billy for everything, Geoffrey. What would he want with it?
GEOFFREY	*(Indicating the papers on the floor.)* What's he want with this bloody lot? There's neither sense nor bloody reason in him. And where is he, anyway? Where's he taken himself off to?

element of truth.

ALICE	I don't know, Geoffrey. I've given up caring.
GEOFFREY	You'd think he could stay in one bloody night of the year. He ought to be in tonight. He ought to be in looking after his mother. He's got no sense of bloody responsibility, that's his trouble.

20

ALICE	Well, she liked her cup of tea. We'll have that pint-pot to put away now. She's used that pint-pot for as long as I can remember.
GEOFFREY	She liked her bloody tea, there's no getting away from it. *(He half-jokes in an attempt to lift ALICE out of her depression.)* If I had a shilling for every pot of tea she's supped I'd be a rich man today. Well, there's one good thing to be said for it, when does the dustbin man come around? 'Cause he can take all them tins of condensed milk out of her bedroom.

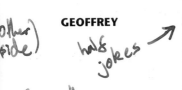

Other side)

half jokes ➚

Sympathy

30

ALICE	We can't throw them away. Somebody might be glad of them. We could send them round to the Old People's Home, or something.
GEOFFREY	Get away with you, you'd poison the bloody lot of them. That stuff doesn't keep for ever you know. They'll be green mouldy.
ALICE	I thought it was supposed to keep – condensed milk.
GEOFFREY	It won't keep twenty bloody years, I'm sure. She's had that pile of tins stacked up there since nineteen thirty-nine. And there's not one of them been opened – not one.

keeps things

— isted apart.

40

ALICE	Well, they went scarce, Geoffrey, when the war started, you know. That's why she started saving them.

GEOFFREY	Went scarce? Too bloody true they went scarce, she had them all. She hoarded them – she was like a squirrel with them. If Lord Woolton had heard about her in nineteen forty-one she'd have got fifteen years. By bloody hell, she would. *(He reminisces gently.)* Hey! I say! Do you remember how I used to pull her leg about it? How I used to tell her the Food Office was ringing up for her? You couldn't get her near that bloody telephone. She used to let it ring when we were out – she must have lost me pounds.
ALICE	*(Not cheered by GEOFFREY'S attempt at humour.)* Well, I only hope you manage as well when you're as old as she was. She's not had an easy life – I wish I could have made it easier for her. She had all us to bring up, you know. And that took some doing.
GEOFFREY	No – she didn't do too bad, to say. What was she? Eighty-what?
ALICE	She'd have been eighty-three in August. Either eighty-three or eighty-two. She didn't seem to know herself.
GEOFFREY	Well, I shan't grumble if I last as long – she had a fair old crack of the whip.
ALICE	She didn't suffer, that's something to be grateful for. Some of them hang on for months and months. What did you say she was talking about? Before she went?
GEOFFREY	Don't ask me. I couldn't hear for that bloody shambles that was going on down here. I've never heard anything like it in all my born days.
ALICE	Well, you can blame our Billy for that, because I do. I've not finished with that Rita-whatever-her-name-is. I shall

50

60

70

Lord Woolton . . . the Food Office . . . *Lord Woolton was in charge of the ministry of food during the war when hoarding was a crime. Florence seems to have been hoarding tinned milk since the war started in 1939.*

77

	find out where she lives. I shall go round and I shall find out.
GEOFFREY	I know her. She works in that milk-bar in Sheepgate. I know her and I know her bloody father as well. You know him. Him that's always racing that whippet on the moor. Him with them tattoos all up his arms. Supposed to work in the market, when he does work. They live in them terrace-houses. Down Mill Lane.
ALICE	Well, I shall go round. I shall go round and see her mother.
GEOFFREY	You'll go bloody nowhere. You keep away. We've got enough to cope with without getting mixed up with that lot.
ALICE	I only wish she could have been spared it. If you can't die in peace, what can you do?
GEOFFREY	You don't want to go fretting yourself about that. She heard nothing about it. She was miles away.
ALICE	And what do you say she said? Did she know you?
GEOFFREY	Well, she did at first. She was all right after you went down. And she was all right when our Billy came up with her medicine. She took that all right and kept it down. She was just ramblin' on – like she does. She was chuntering on about a tin of salmon going to waste. Then something about getting her pension book changed at the post office next week. She never knew, you see. It was just this last five minutes when she started to slaver. I was holding her up in bed and she just slumped forward. I thought she was having a bloody fit. But no – she just gave a little jerk with her head – like that. Then she started to slaver. She was just like a baby, Alice. Just like a baby, slavering and gasping for

Handwritten annotation: sympathy / pain

80

90

100

slaver *'dribble'*

breath. She wet my handkerchief through, I know that. Then she sits straight up – by herself – and says, 'Where's my Jack?' I had to think who she was talking about. Then I remembered she must have meant your father. Only she always used to call him John, didn't she?

ALICE   *(Half to herself.)* She hardly ever called him Jack.

GEOFFREY   Then she said, 'I love you, Jack'. Oh, and before she said, 'What are you thinking about?' – she must have been talking to your father, she couldn't have been talking to anyone else. But you had to listen close to, to hear what she 110 was saying. She could hardly speak. By the time she went she couldn't speak at all. She was just slavering.

pathos
sad

There is a pause.

ALICE   You should have called me.

GEOFFREY   *(Suddenly compassionate.)* She wouldn't have known you. And you wouldn't have liked to have seen her like that. You couldn't have done anything for her – nobody could.

ALICE   You should have called me, Geoffrey.   *tenderness*

GEOFFREY   I didn't think it would have done you any good to see her, that's all. *(Reverting to his normal tones.)* And, listen! If he 120 thinks he's going to the funeral in them bloody suede shoes, he's got another think coming. There'll be all them Masonics coming – I'm not having him showing me up. He'll get some bloody black ones or stop at home.

ALICE   He's got some black ones but he won't wear them.

GEOFFREY   Well, make him. And think on and see that he gets a bloody good wash on Tuesday morning. When did he have a bath last?

Masonics *Freemasons: members of a society (which Geoffrey wants to impress).*

think on and . . . *'Make sure that . . .'*

ALICE	Well, there'll be no baths on Tuesday, 'cause I'm not lighting any fires – I shall be too busy. And I still know nothing about the funeral. I wish I'd have seen Mr Duxbury.

130

GEOFFREY	You only just missed him. If you'd have gone to your Emily's five minutes later you would have seen him. Anyway, they're doing everything. Shadrack and Duxbury's. He says they'll fix the tea for us – the lot.

ALICE	And you still haven't told me what Mr Duxbury said about our Billy – about him getting into bother at work.

GEOFFREY	Don't talk to me about our Billy. I'm going to start putting him in the coal cellar when people come. Duxbury comes to the door – I take him straight upstairs. He starts measuring her up so I left him to it. Come down here and walk into the living-room and there's bloody Dopey sat in here. He's let the fire go out. Kettle boiling it's bloody head off. He's sitting with his shoes and socks off and all muck between his toes watching bloody Noddy on television. *(Losing his temper.)* His grandmother bloody dead upstairs and all he can do is watch Noddy.

140

escape reality
of death

ALICE	I can't understand him. He doesn't seem to have any feeling for anybody.

150

WRITING: What has happened between Act 2 and Act 3? In pairs, write the scene where Geoffrey finds the calendars.

WRITING: Write the obituary that a local reporter might have written after Florence's death.

DISCUSSION: As a class, discuss what Geoffrey's account of Florence's death reveals about him.

Stradhoughton Echo

OBITUARIES

Octagenarian dies quietly at her daughter's home.

The death occured recently of Florence Boothroyd. She was the mother of Alice Fisher and had lived at her daughter's home with her son-in-law and their son, Billy

GEOFFREY

Meant to be at work.

I told him. I said to him, 'What are you bloody doing? Do you know Mr Duxbury's upstairs?' He was out of that chair and through that door like a shot. I watched him out of our bedroom window – putting his shoes and socks on in the street. I'll bloody swing for him before I've finished, I will.

ALICE Well, what did Mr Duxbury say about him?

GEOFFREY He wasn't going to say anything. Not today. Until I asked him if our Billy had rung up and asked for his cards, like he said he was. Then the lot came out. *(He indicates the calendars.)* There's all these calendars he's supposed to have posted, for one. Then there's his petty cash – that doesn't add up. Then there's his postage book. Two pound ten postage money he's had. And he's supposed to have pinched a brass plate off a coffin. What does he want to do a bloody trick like that for? 160

ALICE You didn't say anything about postage money before – you just said petty cash.

GEOFFREY I don't know. Don't ask me. The whole bloody lot's wrong from start to finish. He can't keep his hands off nothing.

ALICE But what did he say about not taking him to court? 170

GEOFFREY How many more bloody times? He says if he stays on – and does his work right, and pays this money back – and stops giving back-chat every five minutes – he'll hear no more about it.

ALICE But what about him going to London?

GEOFFREY How the bloody hell can he go to London? He'll go to Dartmoor if he's not careful. He's to stop on there until he's

Dartmoor *A famous prison in Devon.*

81

paid this money back – and I know I'm not paying it, if he goes down on his bended knees I'm not paying it.

ALICE   It's a mystery to me why he wanted to take that money in the first place. He never buys anything – and if he does go short he knows he's only to come to me.   180

GEOFFREY   You've been too soft with him, that's been the bloody trouble, all along. Anyway, you know what he's spent it on, don't you? That bloody engagement ring. That's where the money's gone. Well, he can get that back to the shop for a start. And he can get engaged when he's twenty-one and not before. And he brings no more bloody lasses round here. And he comes in at nine o'clock in future – never mind half-past eleven. There's going to be some changes in   190 this house.

harsh →

ALICE   Yes, and you've said that before and it's made no difference. He used to get on her nerves.

GEOFFREY   Well, she's not got him to put up with any more. He used to lead her a dog's life. I've seen him – mocking her. And where is he? He's got no bloody right to be out.

ALICE   I don't know where he's got to.

GEOFFREY   *obsession →* He'll know where he's got to when he rolls in here. He'll go straight out again – through the bloody window.

ALICE   We don't want any more rows tonight, Geoffrey. My nerves won't stand it. You've had one row today and you saw what happened. She was all right till you started on our Billy.   200

GEOFFREY   Don't start bloody blaming me for it. For God's sake. I told her often enough to go to see that doctor.

ALICE   You know very well she wouldn't go.

GEOFFREY   It was your bloody job to see that she did. I'm not on tap twenty-four hours a bloody day. I've got work to do.

They are building up to an argument.

82

tension

ALICE	And I've got my work to do as well. I did my best. I tried to make her go. You know why it was. It was because he was black. 210
GEOFFREY	I don't care if he was sky-blue bloody pink with yellow dots on. You should have gone with her.
ALICE	*(Almost in tears.)* It was only this afternoon she was sitting in that chair with a pot of tea. You can say what you like, she was all right till you started on to our Billy.
GEOFFREY	She was never all right. She hadn't been all right for bloody months.
ALICE	It's tomorrow morning I'm thinking about. When I should be taking her up her pot of tea and a Marie Louise biscuit. 220
GEOFFREY	Will you shut up about bloody pots of tea! You won't fetch her back with pots of bloody tea. She'll get no pots of tea where she's gone.
ALICE	Well, I like to think she will! *(She rises and crosses towards the kitchen.)*
GEOFFREY	Where are you going now?
ALICE	I'm going to make myself one.
GEOFFREY	Sit you down, I'll see to it.
ALICE	No. No. I'm better when I'm doing something. I'd rather be occupied. 230
	ALICE goes into the kitchen and GEOFFREY crosses to join her.
GEOFFREY	I'll give you a hand, anyway.

DISCUSSION: As a class, discuss whether you agree with Alice's statement that Billy 'doesn't seem to have any feeling for anybody.'

WRITING: 'You've been too soft with him . . .'. What is the best way to handle Billy? Write some advice to Billy's parents, as though from an agony aunt (or uncle).

lack of communication. with parents.

GEOFFREY goes into the kitchen as the lights fade down in the living-room. The lights come up in the garden – both from the porch and the street lamp. We discover BILLY sitting on the garden seat, rather cold and his hands dug deep in his pockets. He lights a cigarette, then rises and crosses to the front door where he listens for a moment through the letter box. Hearing nothing he returns towards the garden seat and sits disconsolately. 240

Lonelyness

Imaginary

Mx is ...

BILLY

powerfull

BILLY hums to himself and then turns on the seat and takes up a garden cane. He toys with the cane for a moment, attempting to balance it on his fingers. His humming grows louder and he stands and conducts an imaginary orchestra using the cane as a baton. He is humming a military march and he suddenly breaks off as the garden cane becomes, in his imagination, a rifle. He shoulders the cane and marches briskly up and down the garden path.

(Marching.) Lef', ri', lef', ri', lef'-ri'-lef'! Halt! *(He halts.)* Order arms! *(He brings the cane down to the 'Order' position.)* 250

He pauses for a moment and the garden cane becomes, in his imagination, an officer's baton which he tucks under his arm and then he marches smartly off to an imaginary saluting base a few paces away. He has become, in his imagination, a major-general. — escapist

Status

Mixture of fantasy + Reality

STATUS

Dearly beloved Officers and Gentlemen of the Desert Shock Troops. We are assembled at the grave-side here this evening to pay our respects to a great lady. There are many of us here tonight who would not be alive now but for her tender mercies although in her later years she was limbless 260 from the waist down. She struggled valiantly to combat ignorance and disease. Although she will be remembered by

disconsolately *'in a mood where he cannot be cheered up'* the world as the inventor of penicillin and radium we, of this proud regiment, will remember her as our friend – the Lady of the Lamp. I call upon you all to join with me in observing two minutes' silence.

BILLY removes an imaginary hat which he places under his arm. He lowers his head respectfully and stands in silence. Imitating a bugle he hums the 'Last Post'. He is still standing, his head lowered, as ARTHUR and LIZ enter the garden. Although LIZ is about the same age as BARBARA and RITA she has more maturity and self-possession. Although she is dressed casually and is, in fact, wearing the black skirt we have heard so much about, she is not as scruffy as we have been led to believe. She is also wearing a white blouse and a green suede jacket. She is not particularly pretty but is obviously a girl of strong personality. LIZ is the only girl for whom BILLY has any real feelings. LIZ and ARTHUR stand for a moment looking at BILLY, who has not noticed them.

270

280

290

ARTHUR   What's up with him, then?

?   **the inventor of penicillin and radium . . .** *In Billy's fantasy, his grandmother becomes Alexander Fleming, Marie Curie and Florence Nightingale rolled into one.*

Handwritten margin notes: "Clearly is Upset", "Liz is the only one who he has feelings for", "imaginary comic", "sadness & death", "feelings for", "feelings 4 Bab + Rita are only pretended.", "Feelings for a Liz"

BILLY	*(Startled and embarrassed.)* I didn't hear you coming . . . *(He sees LIZ for the first time and is even more embarrassed.)* Liz.
LIZ	Hallo, Billy.
ARTHUR	What are you on, then? He's saying his prayers.
BILLY	*(He scratches the ground with the cane with an assumed casualness.)* No, I was just standing. Just thinking to myself. *(To LIZ.)* Arthur told me you were back. 300
ARTHUR has no sympathy anymore	You look like one of them stinking gnomes we've got in our garden. With a maring fishing rod. *(BILLY tosses the garden cane into the garden.)* What are you standing out here for? Won't they let you in?
BILLY	*(Irritated.)* Can't I stand in my own rotten garden now? *(To LIZ.)* When did you get back?
LIZ	Last week.
ARTHUR	*(Before she can continue.)* Hey, is it right your grandma's snuffed it?
BILLY	You what? Yes. This afternoon. Funeral's on Tuesday. 310
ARTHUR	Fizzing hell! I was only talking to her this morning.
BILLY	*(To LIZ.)* Why didn't you ring up?
ARTHUR	*(Before she can reply.)* You don't half drop me in it! I thought you'd made it up. I told our old lady you'd made it up! She'll go stinking bald.
BILLY has a big head	*(To LIZ.)* You've got the number. You could have rung me up.
LIZ	I was going to, Billy.
ARTHUR	*(Again before she can continue.)* Do you know what I was going to do? If I'd had enough money. I was going to send 320 a wreath round. With a little card saying in capital letters: 'You Stinking Louse-bound Crowing Liar'. I was sure you'd made it up.

BILLY	*(Annoyed.)* What are you talking about? What would I want to make up a thing like that for?
ARTHUR	Oh, get George Washington. *(In a mimicking falsetto.)* Please sir, I cannot tell a lie. I chopped up Grandma.
BILLY	*(Turning to ARTHUR.)* Look, why don't you just jack it in – eh?
ARTHUR	All right, all right. Keep your shirt on. Don't go biting my head off. 330
BILLY	Well, you want to grow up.
ARTHUR	You what! Listen who's talking. You're a right one to talk. Grow up? Blimey! *(He turns to LIZ.)* Do you know what he once did? He saves up these plastic boats you get out of cornflake packets. He does! He saves them all. He keeps them in his desk. Well, do you know what he once did? He filled up a baby's coffin with water – down in the basement – and started playing at naval battles. He thinks I don't know. 340
BILLY	Aw, shut up. Anyway, I don't sit in the lavatory all morning. Reading mucky books.
ARTHUR	No, and I don't go around playing at Winston Churchills when I think nobody's looking.
BILLY	Aw, belt up, man!
ARTHUR	*(Tapping BILLY on the chest.)* You just want to stop telling people to belt up. You want to go careful, man. Or else somebody's going to belt you.

> **?** Oh, get George Washington . . . *In a famous story, the 18th Century US President, as a child, owned up to chopping down a tree, with the words 'I cannot tell a lie . . .'.*
>
> **jack it in** *'pack it in'; 'stop it'*
>
> **playing Winston Churchills** *Churchill, leader of Britain during World War II*

BILLY	Yeh – you and whose army?
ARTHUR	I'm not talking about me. I'm talking about somebody else. 　350
BILLY	Who?
ARTHUR	Somebody's brother.
BILLY	Whose naffing brother? What are you talking about?
ARTHUR	Rita's naffing brother. Who do you think? That's what I came up to tell you – thanks very much for asking. It's the last favour I'll do you, I know that. I've just seen him down at the dance hall. Screaming blue murder. I wouldn't like to be in your shoes, man, when he gets you.
BILLY	*(Uneasily.)* I'm not frightened of him.
ARTHUR	You what! He'll bloody slaughter you. He will, you know, 　360 he's not kidding.
BILLY	So what.
ARTHUR	So what, he says. I knew you should never have given her that ring in the first place. I told you, didn't I? Well, she still wants it back, you know. You've had your chips.
BILLY	Aaahh – who cares.
ARTHUR	You'll bloody care when you're in the infirmary getting stitched up. Well, you've had it coming, matey, let's face it. You and your rotten lying. Well, I know what I'd do if I was you – and I didn't want to get crippled. I'd get off to that 　370 job in London, dead smartish – that's if there is a job in London.
BILLY	What do you mean – if there is a job in London?
ARTHUR	I mean, if it isn't another of your stinking lies!

Handwritten margin notes: "AGGRESSION - BREWING"; "violence"

> **?** infirmary *'hospital'*

Athar not playing games any more not tolerating lies any more

BILLY	I'll go – don't you worry.
ARTHUR	I'm not worrying, Tosh. I've got more to do with my time. But I'll tell you this much, you can stop going round giving out the patter about our old lady. Because if I hear – once more – about her being in the family way, I'll be round here myself. Never mind Rita's brother.

380

BILLY	Aw – dry up. *He's not p*
ARTHUR	*(Going off.)* Well, I've told you, man. *(He turns to BILLY.)* And don't think I'm covering up for you any more – 'cause I'm not.
BILLY	*(Softly.)* Aw – get knotted.
	ARTHUR goes. BILLY turns to LIZ.
	He talks too much. *(There is a slight pause as they stand and look at each other.)* . . . Hallo, Liz.
LIZ	Hallo, Billy. *greeting!*
BILLY	When did you get back?

390

LIZ	Last week.
BILLY	Why didn't you ring me up?
LIZ	I was going to.
BILLY	Thank you very much.

? **giving out the patter** *'telling entertaining stories'*

ACTING: In threes, act out the scene from Billy's entrance on page 84 to Liz's 'Hello, Billy.' on page 86.

HOT-SEATING: Hot-seat Arthur. Ask him how his attitude to Billy has changed since the beginning of the play.

LIZ	No – really. I was going to. I thought I'd see you at the dance tonight. I went to the dance. I thought you'd be there. *Boosh*
BILLY	I couldn't go.
LIZ	No. No – I know. I heard about your grandma. I'm sorry.
BILLY	Yes. *(Changing the subject.)* I haven't seen you for months. **400**
LIZ	Five weeks. You didn't waste much time, did you?
BILLY	Why? What do you mean?
LIZ	Getting engaged. To everybody.
BILLY	Oh – that. *Shits + giggles*
LIZ	You're mad.
BILLY	*(He shrugs his shoulders.)* Where have you been?
LIZ	Oh – here and there.
BILLY	Why didn't you write?
LIZ	I did – once. I tore it up.
BILLY	You're always tearing it up. **410**
LIZ	*(Changing the subject.)* How's everything with you? How's the script-writing? How's the book coming along?
BILLY	*(Enthusiastically.)* Oh, I've finished it. It's going to be published next Christmas. *(She gives him a long, steady look.)* I haven't started writing it yet.
LIZ	You are mad.
BILLY	Yes. *(LIZ sits on the garden seat.)* Liz?
LIZ	Mmmm?
BILLY	*(Sitting beside her.)* Do you find life complicated?
LIZ	Mmmm. So-so. **420**

Handwritten margin notes:
- we only got engaged because of his absence of Liz
- Just Fun.
- Boosh
- got engaged D A f T
- entirely lies
- Lie, not fantasy Boosh
- First time he doesn't Lie
- Real communication.

BILLY *[language]* I wish it was something you could tear up and start again. Life, I mean. You know – like starting a new page in an exercise book.

LIZ Well, its been done. Turning over a new leaf. *[Sadness + failure]*

BILLY I turn over a new leaf every day – but the blots show through.

LIZ What's all this about London?

BILLY I've been offered a job down there. *[Booth]*

LIZ Honestly?

BILLY Honestly. A sort of job.   430

LIZ Good, I'm glad. Perhaps it's your new leaf.

BILLY *(Proud of the phrase.)* I turn over a new leaf every day – but the blots show through the page.

LIZ Well, perhaps a new leaf isn't good enough. Perhaps you need to turn over a new volume. *[Crap. — pause]*

BILLY Yes. *[Doughts]*

LIZ Are you going to take that job?

BILLY I think so.

LIZ You only think so? *[Uncertenly]*

BILLY I don't know.   440

LIZ You know, my lad, the trouble with you is that you're – what's the word? – introspective. You're like a child at the edge of a paddling pool. You want very much to go in, but you think so much about whether the water's cold, and

[looking inwards.]   *[She understands him]*

> **?** **introspective** *Liz thinks that Billy examines his own thoughts and feelings too much.*

whether you'll drown, and what your mother will say if you get your feet wet . . .

BILLY   *(Interrupting.)* All I'm doing is wondering whether to dive or swim.

LIZ   Perhaps you need a coach.

BILLY   Do you know why I'm so fascinated by London?   450

LIZ   No. Why?

BILLY   A man can lose himself in London. London is a big place. It has big streets – and big people.

[handwritten: Fantasy / STATUS]

[handwritten beside BILLY: goes inside his own head.]

LIZ   *(Giving him another look.)* Mad.

[handwritten: Doesn't solve anything]

BILLY   Perhaps I need to turn over a new paddling pool.

There is a pause as they look at each other.

LIZ   Who do you love?

BILLY   *(Adopting his thick north country accent.)* Thee, lass.

LIZ   Yes, it sounds like it, doesn't it?

BILLY   I do, lass.   460

LIZ   Say it properly, then.

BILLY   I do, Liz. I do.

[handwritten: Afraid]

LIZ   What about Barbara?

BILLY   Well, what about her?

LIZ   Well, *what* about her?

BILLY   All over. *[handwritten: Boosh]*

LIZ   You've said that before.

[handwritten: LOVE]

[handwritten right margin: only shares this with Liz not Barb or Rita]

     A man can lose himself in London . . . *More romantic film dialogue.*

Thee lass *Billy puts on a joke accent to avoid having to answer seriously.*

BILLY	I know. This time it is all over.
LIZ	And what about the other one? Rita-whatever-her-name-is?
BILLY	That's all over, too. B oo s h

470

There is a pause. BILLY takes out a packet of cigarettes, lights two and gives one to LIZ.

LIZ	I want to marry you, you know, Billy. ├ WHY)
BILLY	I know, Liz – I know. We will – one day. procrastination
LIZ	Not one day. Now.
BILLY Imp	Do you?
LIZ	Next week will do. Before you go to London. Or when you get there. Whichever you prefer.
BILLY	I think I get engaged a bit too often.
LIZ	I don't want to get engaged. I want to get married.

480

BILLY	Is that why you keep sloping off every few weeks? Because you want to get married?
LIZ	I want to get married.
BILLY	All right. All right.
LIZ	How do you mean – all right? I've just proposed to you and you say 'all right'. Aren't you supposed to say 'this is so sudden' or 'yes' or something.
BILLY	I don't know. Indisisive , unable to take effective action

LIZ puts her arms round him and kisses him. He responds. They break away.

490

LIZ	Billy?
BILLY	Yes?
LIZ	You know what you wanted me to do? That night? When we walked through the park? And I said 'another night'?

BILLY I remember.

LIZ Well, it's another night tonight, isn't it?

BILLY *LOVE* (*Afraid but excited.*) Are you sure?

OH WOW

LIZ Yes.   ~~Hot & Steamy~~

BILLY Where could we go?

LIZ I've got a room. There's no one there.   **500**

BILLY What do you think we ought to do about – you know,
babies.

LIZ Have them. Lots and lots of them.

BILLY No, I mean tonight.   *Yes tonight!*

LIZ It's all right. (*After a pause.*) Billy?

2 yong people trying to understand each other and life

BILLY Yes?

LIZ Ask you something?

BILLY What?

Virgin ~~register~~!

LIZ Do you know what *virgo intacta* means?

BILLY Yes.   **510**

LIZ Well, I'm not.   *Feburary 28*

BILLY No. I somehow didn't think you were.

LIZ Want me to tell you about it?

BILLY No. (*He kisses her.*) All right, yes. Tell me about it.

LIZ No – not now.

BILLY Tell me about it.

  Virgo intacta *This is a medical term meaning 'virgin'.*

You think that's why I'm always going away . . . *either to have*
abortions or to visit a distant lover

Rita is a slut!   slut!
slut! slut!

LIZ	You think that's why I'm always going away, don't you?
BILLY	I don't know.
LIZ	Ask me where I've been for the past five weeks.
BILLY	What difference does it make?
LIZ	None – I suppose. It's just that every so often I want to go away. It's not you, Billy. I want to be here with you. It's the town. It's the people we know. I don't like knowing everybody – or becoming a part of things. Do you see what I mean?
BILLY	Yes . . . yes.
LIZ	What I'd like is to be invisible. You know, to be able to move around without people knowing, and not having to worry about them. Not having to explain all the time.
BILLY	Liz . . . Liz! Listen! Listen! Liz, do you know what I do? When I want to feel invisible. I've never told anybody. I have a sort of – well, it's an imaginary country. Where I go. It has its own people . . .
LIZ	(Interrupting.) Do you do that? I knew you would. Why are we so alike, Billy? I can read your thoughts. A town like this. Only somewhere over by the sea. And we used to spend the whole day on the beach. That's what I used to think about.
BILLY	This is more than a town – it's a whole country. (He is getting excited.) I'm supposed to be the Prime Minister. You're supposed to be the Foreign Secretary – or something.
LIZ	(With mock obedience.) Yes, sir.
BILLY	I think about it for hours. Sometimes I think, if we were married, with a house of our own, we could just sit and imagine ourselves there.
LIZ	Yes, we could.

530

540

[handwritten margin notes:] She wants to escape the limitations of a small town but through a proper and full relationship

[handwritten note:] he wants to live in his imagination

Screech

BILLY   I want a room, in the house, with a green baize door. It will be a big room, and when we go into it, through the door, that's it, that's our country. No one else would be allowed in. No one else will have keys. They won't know where the room is. Only we'll know. And we'll make models of the principal cities. You know, out of cardboard. And we could use toy soldiers. Painted. For the people. We could draw maps. It would be a place to go to on a rainy afternoon. We could go there. No one would find us. I thought we could have a big sloping shelf running all the way down one wall, you know, like a big desk. And we'd have a lot of blank paper on it and design our own newspapers. We could even make uniforms, if we wanted to. It would be our country . . . *(He falters away.)*   550

560

His world

LIZ   Let's have a model train that the kids won't be allowed to use.

BILLY   Liz . . .? Will you marry me? — *whaaat*

LIZ   Yes. *(He kisses her.)* Billy?

BILLY   Yes?

LIZ   Are you really going to London or just pretending?

BILLY   I'm thinking about it.

won't commit to action

96

LIZ	Only thinking?
BILLY	Well, going. Soon, anyway.
LIZ	When's soon?
BILLY	Well, soon.
LIZ	That's a bit vague. Soon. Why not now?
BILLY	It's difficult.
LIZ	No, it's easy. You just get on a train and four hours later there you are – in London.
BILLY	It's easy for you, you've had the practice.
LIZ	I'll come with you.
BILLY	That'd be marvellous – if we could.
LIZ	*(She rises.)* But we can, Billy! We can! What is there to stop us?
BILLY	*(Thinking seriously about it for the first time.)* Well, there's . . . I don't know . . . you've got to make all sorts of arrangements, haven't you?
LIZ	You buy a ticket, that's all. You buy a ticket and get on a train. That's all there is to it.
BILLY	I've never thought about it like that.
LIZ	Billy, we can! We can go! We can go tonight!
BILLY	But, Liz.
LIZ	There's the midnight train. We can catch that. It gets in at

Handwritten annotations:
Practical motivation — 570
She has dreams but determination
he wont like the plunge.
580

DISCUSSION: In pairs, look back through the play and find the places where Billy uses humour to get himself out of trouble or to avoid having to make a serious response.

DISCUSSION: As a class, discuss what Billy's and Liz's creation of a fantasy land tells you about them.

	King's Cross Station. Breakfast at Lyons Corner House. Then we get a tube – we get a tube from Piccadilly Circus to Earl's Court. I've got friends there, Billy. They'll put us up. They'd give us a room. **590**
BILLY	*(Almost convinced. He rises.)* Tonight, Liz?
LIZ	Yes, tonight! Twelve-five from New Street Station. We'll be in London tomorrow. We can go to Hyde Park in the afternoon. We'll go to the pictures tomorrow night – the Odeon, Marble Arch. What time is it now?
BILLY	*(Glancing at his watch.)* Just after ten.
LIZ	I'm going, Billy. Are you coming? **600**
BILLY	*(His mind made up.)* Yes, Liz. I'm coming.
LIZ	Are you sure?
BILLY	I'm coming with you.
LIZ	*(Briskly.)* Right, then. I'm going home. Now. And I'm going to pack my things. I'll meet you at the station. In that refreshment room. In an hour's time. Eleven o'clock. I'll get the tickets. Two singles to London. You won't let me down, Billy?
BILLY	I'm coming.
LIZ	What will you tell your father and mother? **610**
BILLY	They know already – more or less.
LIZ	You won't let them talk you out of it?
BILLY	I'm coming.
	The lights begin to come up in the living-room. GEOFFREY

Lyons Corner House *This was a popular chain of cafés.*

a tube *the London Underground*

enters from the kitchen, takes up a newspaper, sits down and begins to read. The lights fade slightly in the garden.

620

LIZ   *(She kisses BILLY.)* Eleven o'clock.

BILLY   Eleven.

LIZ goes off down the garden. BILLY watches her go and then turns and enters the house. GEOFFREY rises at the sound of the

630

door. BILLY enters the living-room. He registers shock as he sees that his cupboard has been opened.

GEOFFREY   What time of bloody night do you call this?

BILLY   It's only ten.

GEOFFREY   I don't care what bloody time it is. Who said you could go out? And where've you been?

BILLY   I've only been out. Why? Did you want some chips bringing in?

GEOFFREY   I'll chip you. I'll chip you round your bloody ear-hole if I   640
               start on you. Have you been out dancing?

BILLY   No, 'course I haven't.

Violence

VIOLENCE

HOT-SEATING: In groups of four, hot-seat Billy and ask him what went through his head (a) as he was going through the front door; (b) when he saw that the cupboard had been opened.

he loves

GEOFFREY If you've been out dancing with your grandma lying dead I'll bloody murder you, I will.

BILLY *(Feigning innocence)* What's up?

GEOFFREY What's up – you know what's up. What have you done with that letter of your mother's?

BILLY glances in fear at the envelopes on the floor.

Do you hear me? I'm talking to you!

BILLY What letter? 650

GEOFFREY What, what, what! Don't keep saying bloody 'what'. You know what letter. That what she gave you to post to 'Housewives' Choice'.

BILLY I told her once. I posted it.

GEOFFREY *(Taking the letter from his pocket.)* You posted bloody nothing. You've had it in that cupboard. It was given to you to post. You bloody idle little swine.

BILLY I did post it. That's just the rough copy.

GEOFFREY What are you talking about? Rough copy? It's your mother's letter. How could you have posted it? 660

BILLY Look – the letter my mother wrote was full of mistakes, that's all. I just thought it would stand a better chance if I wrote it out again – properly. That's all.

ALICE enters from the kitchen.

GEOFFREY Well, who told you to write it out again? And who told you to open it? You keep your thieving hands off other people's things! And where did you get all them bloody calendars from, as well?

BILLY What calendars?

GEOFFREY *(Fingering his belt.)* By bloody hell! I'll give you 'what' if you don't' stop saying 'what, what', my lad! You know what! 670

Don't think I haven't been talking to Mr Duxbury – because I have. I've heard it all. You make me a laughing-stock. You can't keep your hands off nothing. And where's that monkey wrench out of my garage? I suppose you know nothing about that?

BILLY   No, 'course I don't. What do I want with a monkey wrench?

GEOFFREY   What do you want with two hundred bloody calendars! And what have you been doing with their name-plates as   680 well? You're not right in the bloody head.

BILLY   (*Losing his temper.*) I'm not right! I'm not right! I didn't want to work for Shadrack and flaming Duxbury's! You made me take the rotten job! Now you can answer for it.

GEOFFREY   Don't bloody shout at me, you gormless young get – or I'll knock your eyes out.

BILLY   God give me strength.

GEOFFREY   Give you strength, he wants to give you some sense! You're like a bloody Mary-Ann! Well, I hope your mother gets more sense out of you.   690

ALICE   Well, you've got yourself into a fine mess, lad, haven't you?

BILLY   Have I?

ALICE   I'm only thankful she knows nothing about it. (*She glances up at the ceiling.*) Why didn't you post that letter of mine?

BILLY   I did post it. I was telling Dad. I just wrote it out again, that's all. There was some mistakes in it.

? **Fingering his belt** *He is about to hit Billy.*

gormless 'stupid'

a bloody Mary-Ann *It says much of Geoffrey that one of the worst things that he can say about his son is that he is like a girl.*

ALICE *(crying)*	Yes, well we can't all be Shakespeares, can we? And what's all this about you taking money from work?
BILLY *(laugh)*	What money?
GEOFFREY	*(Warningly.)* I've told you.
BILLY	What? I haven't taken any money.
GEOFFREY	There's two pound ten short in your postage book. Never mind petty cash.
BILLY	Oh, that . . . I
ALICE	What did you do with it, Billy?
GEOFFREY	He's spent it. That's what he's bloody done with it.
ALICE	Well, it's just beyond me. You didn't have to take money, Billy. You could have come to me.
GEOFFREY	You've had things too bloody easy. That's been your trouble. You can't carry on at work like you do at home, you know.
BILLY	Well, I told you I didn't want to work there when I first started, didn't I?
GEOFFREY	You didn't want to work for nobody, if you ask me anything. You thought you'd live on me, didn't you?
BILLY	No, I didn't. I could have kept myself
ALICE	Kept yourself – how?
BILLY	Writing scripts.
GEOFFREY	Writing bloody scripts, you want to get a day's work done, never mind writing scripts. Who do you think's going to run this bloody business when I'm gone?
BILLY	You said you didn't want me in the business.
GEOFFREY	Only because you were so bloody idle! Somebody's got to carry on with it! Who's going to keep your mother?

700

710

720

BILLY	*(With an attempt at humour.)* Why, you're not retiring, are you?
GEOFFREY	Don't try and be funny with me, lad! Or you'll laugh on the other side of your face!
ALICE	And what did you tell me about Arthur's mother? She wasn't having a baby, you know very well she wasn't. 730
BILLY	It was only a joke.
GEOFFREY	A joke – it sounds like a bloody joke!
ALICE	And why did you tell her I'd broken my leg?
BILLY	I didn't know you knew Arthur's mother.
ALICE	Yes, you don't know who I know and who I don't know, do you? If you want to know, she rang me up. And what did you do with that cardigan she gave you for me, last Christmas?
BILLY	*(Vaguely.)* I think I gave it to the refugees.
ALICE	Well, you've got a new cardigan to find by tomorrow morning. Because she's coming round to see me. 740
BILLY	*(Emphatically.)* I won't be here tomorrow morning.
GEOFFREY	You won't be here to bloody night if you talk to your mother in that tone of voice!
BILLY	I'm not going to be here tonight. I'm leaving.
ALICE	What are you talking about?
BILLY	*(Decisively.)* I'm getting the midnight train. Tonight. I'm taking that job in London.
ALICE	If you're in any more trouble, Billy, it's not something you can leave behind you. You put it in your suitcase and take it with you. 750
GEOFFREY	Well, he's not taking that suitcase of mine upstairs. *(Turning to BILLY.)* Anyway, you're not going to London or nowhere

103

else – so you can get that idea out of your head, for a kick-off.

BILLY   I mean it, Dad. I'm going.

GEOFFREY   And I bloody mean it, as well. *(Raising his voice.)* You stop here till that money's paid back. You can thank your lucky stars Mr Duxbury's not landed you in court. You want to be grateful.   760

BILLY   Grateful! Grateful! Grateful for this, grateful for that! That's all I've heard ever! Grateful you let me go to the grammar school! We've been hearing that one since the first day I went there. What am I supposed to do? Say 'thank you very much' three times a day for my marvellous education?

GEOFFREY ∧.   Well, it's a chance we never had!

BILLY   Yes, and don't we bloody well know it! I even had to be grateful for winning my own scholarship! And what did you say when I came running home to tell you I'd won it? Don't think I've forgotten! I was eleven years old! I came   770
belting out of those school gates and I ran all the way! Just to tell you! And what did you say? That you'd have to pay for the uniform and I'd have to be grateful! And now I'm supposed to be grateful to Shadrack and stinking Duxbury! Why? What for? For letting me sit at one of their rotten desks all day?

ALICE   *(Gently reasoning.)* Well, you took the job, Billy.

GEOFFREY   Yes, and he's stopping there till that money's paid back.

BILLY   I'm not arguing about it. I'm going! *(He crosses towards the door.)*   780

GEOFFREY   Go, then! I've finished with you!

  Well, he's not taking that suitcase of mine . . . *Alice's 'you put it in your suitcase' is used figuratively to mean 'you take your problems with you'. Geoffrey takes it literally.*

WHY DIDN'T HE GO TO LONDON

BILLY enters the hall and moves up the stairs. GEOFFREY crosses to the door and calls after BILLY as he goes into the bedroom.

They'll take you to court, you know! I won't stop them! I'm not paying it back! And don't think you're taking my suitcase!

GEOFFREY crosses back into the living-room and stands silent. ALICE sits in the chair by the fire.

ALICE   Oh, dear me . . . Oh, dear me. ⟶ SAD   790

BILLY enters from the bedroom and charges down the stairs and into the living-room. He is carrying a small battered suitcase. He crosses to the sideboard and, opening a drawer, begins to pack the case with shirts, socks, ties and a pullover. GEOFFREY watches him in silence.

ALICE   *(Concerned.)* What time train do you reckon you're catching?

BILLY   Midnight.

ALICE   Well, what time does it get in?

BILLY   Tomorrow morning.   800

ALICE   And where are you going to live when you get there?

GEOFFREY He'll finish up in the Salvation Army Hostel.

ALICE   *(As BILLY packs a pair of socks.)* All them socks need darning, you know. *(BILLY makes no reply.)* Well, you'll want more than one suit . . . And what about your grandma's funeral on Tuesday?

 Salvation Army *This is an organisation that runs hostels for the homeless.*

BILLY has now placed all his clothing in the case. He stoops and begins to pack the calendars.

GEOFFREY	*(In disbelief.)* What the thump are you packing them bloody calendars for?

810

BILLY	I thought I'd post them.
ALICE	Well, you'll be expected at the funeral, you know.
GEOFFREY	*(Disparagingly.)* He's not going anywhere.
BILLY	*(Slamming the case shut he rises.)* I'm going.

He picks up the case and crosses to the door.

GEOFFREY	*(Half-relenting.)* Don't act so bloody daft.

BILLY pauses for a moment, his hand on the door, caught up in the embarrassment of leaving.

BILLY	Well, I'll write to you then. Soon as I've got fixed up. *(Acutely embarrassed.)* I'm sorry about my grandma.

820

He goes out.

ALICE	Oh, dear me . . . Oh, dear me.
GEOFFREY	They can summons him. I've finished.
ALICE	You'll have to pay it, Geoffrey. Will he be all right on his own?
GEOFFREY	He won't bloody go – he'll be back in five minutes.
ALICE	We know nothing about where he's going and what he's supposed to be doing. Who's that fellow he says he's going to work for. That comedian?
GEOFFREY	I don't bloody know.

830

ALICE	It was in that letter he had in his pocket in that old raincoat.

GEOFFREY crosses and takes the envelope from the raincoat which is hanging in the hall. He returns into the living-room reading the letter to himself as he walks. He then reads the letter aloud to ALICE.

GEOFFREY   'Dear Mr Fisher, Many thanks for the script and gags, I can use some of the gags and pay accordingly. As for my staff job, well I regret to tell you, I do not have staff beside my agent, but several of the boys do work for me, you might be   840 interested in this.

(He pauses.)

Why not call in for a chat next time you are in London? Best of luck and keep writing. Danny Boon.'

ALICE   *(After pause.)* Run down to the station and fetch him back.

GEOFFREY   He's off his bloody rocker.

ALICE   You'll have to stop him, Geoffrey.

GEOFFREY   Nay, he's big enough to look after himself now. He can stand on his own two feet for a change. I've finished. I've done my whack for him.   850

ALICE   I wonder if he's got any money?

GEOFFREY   That's his look-out. It doesn't belong to him if he has. You can depend on that.

ALICE   Oh, dear me . . . Oh, dear me.

GEOFFREY   There's no need for him to starve. He can get a job if he sets his mind to it. And get up in the morning.

ALICE   Well, what's he going to do?

GEOFFREY   He can go clerking – same as here. There's a lot of offices in London. Well, there's one thing certain. I know what I'm going to bloody do: I'm off to bed. I've enough on my plate   860

DISCUSSION: As a class, discuss Danny Boon's letter. How good a script-writer do you think Billy is going to be? What is the likelihood that he will have a career in script-writing?

107

without worrying my head over that one. He can go to hell, he can.

ALICE

Do you want a cup of Ovaltine, or anything?

GEOFFREY

No. You want to get off to bed as well, lass.

ALICE

(Rising.) I always used to take her one up at this time. I'll have to get used to it – not having to.

GEOFFREY

Aye, well . . .

ALICE

Is the back door locked, Geoffrey?

GEOFFREY

I've seen to it.

They cross into the hall. GEOFFREY switches off the light in the living-room and automatically drops the catch on the Yale lock. GEOFFREY follows ALICE up the stairs. As they go up, the porch light fades up and RITA and ARTHUR enter the garden.   870

(With assumed cheerfulness.) Well, he'll come home at holiday times. And happen some week-ends.

GEOFFREY switches out the hall light from the top of the stairs and follows ALICE into the bedroom.

ARTHUR

(With relief as he sees the hall light go out.) They've gone to bed.

RITA

Have a look through the rotten letter-box.   880

ARTHUR

You can see! They've gone to bed. You don't think they're sitting there with no lights on, do you?

RITA

Well, he's not getting out of it – 'cause I shall come round in the morning. Our kid'll come round as well. Our kid'll duff him up. He'll get that ring back.

 our kid *'my brother'*

ARTHUR   You and your kid and the louse-bound ring! Come on, let's get down to Foley Bottoms. Get some snogging hours in.

RITA   He needn't think he's got away with it – 'cause he hasn't. He'll be a stretcher case tomorrow morning. (*She screams up at the bedrooms.*) You'll be a stretcher case tomorrow morning! You wait! You rotten yellow-bellied squint-eyed get! You're nothing else! You closet!

We hear the sound of a window being flung open and ALICE shouting.

ALICE   Get away! Don't you know we've got somebody dead in this house!

We hear the window slammed shut.

RITA   (*Screaming.*) You want to be all rotten dead! You want gassing!

ARTHUR   Shut up, Rita! She knows my mother.

RITA   I don't care.

ARTHUR   They're not worth bothering about. Come on – let's get down to Foley Bottoms. We're just wasting time stuck here.

RITA allows ARTHUR to place his arm around her and pilot her out of the garden.

RITA   Well, we'll be round here first thing tomorrow morning. (*As they go.*) We get up before they do.

ARTHUR and RITA go off. There is a pause and then BILLY enters and walks slowly and dejectedly to the front door. He puts down his case and, taking a key from his pocket, opens the door and enters. He crosses into the living-room and, closing the door

890

900

910

 closet '*lavatory*'

behind him, switches on the light. He stands <u>indecisively</u> for a moment and then crosses and switches on the radio. He crosses to his suitcase and opens it as the sound of a dance-band comes from the radio. He stands for a moment and, as the music continues, he compulsively lifts his hand and begins to conduct. He glances towards the ceiling, wondering if he is making too much noise, then crosses and switches off the radio. He returns to the suitcase which he carries over to the sideboard. He opens his cupboard and is neatly stacking the <u>calendars back into the</u> cupboard, as

THE CURTAIN FALLS

920

Look at my Arrow

back to old routine

acceptance clarking is for him

Sad almost trafic

/\ [3

LOOKING BACK AT THE PLAY . . .

1 DISCUSSION: CASTING THE ROLES

In pairs, discuss which film or television actors you would cast in each of the roles, noting down brief reasons to support your choices. Compare your ideas in a class discussion.

2 ARTWORK AND WRITING: DESIGNING A POSTER

Work in pairs on a poster to advertise a stage, television or film version of *Billy Liar*. First, discuss as a class the words and images that usually appear on posters of this kind.

3 ARTWORK AND WRITING: A THEATRE PROGRAMME

Create a programme for a production of the play in the theatre. Remember to include the cast that you have decided on, as well as a background article on the 1950s.

4 WRITING: A DIARY ENTRY

a) Write a diary entry by either Alice or Geoffrey for the day on which Florence dies. Pick out the key moments for the character on that day.
b) Write Billy's diary for the same day.

5 DISCUSSION: 'I DON'T KNOW WHERE HE'LL END UP.'

As a class, discuss what you think Billy will be doing a) in a year's time, and b) in 20 years' time. Give reasons for your suggestions.

6 WRITING: AN EXTRA SCENE

Write a scene to show what happens when Billy next meets Liz, Barbara, Rita, Mr Duxbury or his parents.

7 DISCUSSION AND WRITING: THE WOMEN

As a class, discuss your opinions of the presentation of Billy's three girl-friends. Do they give a fair representation of women, or are they biased and stereotyped? Write an essay on 'The presentation of the young women in *Billy Liar*'.

8 DISCUSSION AND WRITING: THE CHARACTERS' LANGUAGE

In pairs, look back at the notes made on Florence's and Rita's language. Then make notes on other characters' language, showing in each case how it reveals the kind of person they are, and write an essay on 'Characters and language in *Billy Liar*'.

9 WRITING: WHY DOES BILLY LIE?

Re-read Billy's speech on page 104 and the authors' comment that: 'Beneath the comedy runs the story of an imaginative youth fighting to get out of his complacent, cliché-ridden background.'

Then write an essay entitled 'Why does Billy lie?'.

10 DISCUSSION: ADAPTING FROM NOVEL TO PLAY

In pairs, read the extract (see below) from the novel – written before the play. Discuss what the authors have done in adapting the scene for the stage. It can be found on pages 6 to 7. How much of the dialogue has been kept in, for example? What have they changed? What are the strengths of the two different versions?

The old man looked up from some invoices and said: 'And you can start getting bloody well dressed before you come down in a morning.' So far the dialogue was taking a fairly conventional route and I was tempted to throw in one of the old stand-bys, 'Why do you always begin your sentences with an "And"?' Gran, another dress fanatic who always seemed to be fully and even elaborately attired even at two in the morning when she slunk downstairs after the soda-water, chipped in: 'He wants to burn that raincoat, then he'll have to get dressed of a morning.' One of Gran's peculiarities, and she had many, was that she would never address anyone directly but always went through an intermediary, if necessary some static object such as a cupboard. Doing the usual decoding I gathered that she was addressing my mother and that he who should burn the raincoat was the old man, and he who would have to get dressed of a morning was me. 'I gather,' I began, 'that he who should burn the raincoat -' but the old man interrupted:

'And what bloody time did you get in last night? If you can call it last night. This bloody morning, more like.'

I sliced the top off my boiled egg, which in a centre favouring tapping the top with a spoon and peeling the bits off was always calculated to annoy, and said lightly: 'I don't know.'Bout half past eleven, quarter to twelve.'

The old man said: 'More like one o'clock, with your half past bloody eleven! Well you can bloody well and start coming in of a night-time. I'm not having you gallivanting round at all hours, not at your bloody age.'

'Who are you having gallivanting round, then?' I asked, the wit rising for the day like a pale and watery sun.

My mother took over, assuming the clipped, metallic voice of the morning interrogation. 'What were you doing down Foley Bottoms at nine o'clock last night?'

I said belligerently: 'Who says I was down at Foley Bottoms?'

'Never mind who says, or who doesn't say. You were there, and it wasn't that Barbara you were with, neither.'

'He wants to make up his mind who he is going with,' Gran said.

There was a rich field of speculation for me here. Since my mother had never even met the Witch – the one to whom she referred by her given name of Barbara – or Rita either – the one involved in the Foley Bottoms episode, that is – I wondered how she managed to get her hands on so many facts without actually hiring detectives.

I said: 'Well you want to tell whoever saw me to mind their own fizzing business.'

'It is our business,' my mother said. 'And don't you be so cheeky!' I pondered over the absent friend who had supplied the Foley Bottoms bulletin. Mrs Olmonroyd? Ma Walker? Stamp? The Witch herself? I had a sudden hideous notion that the Witch was in league with my mother and that they were to spring some dreadful coup upon me the following day when, with a baptism of lettuce and pineapple chunks, the Witch was due to be introduced to the family at Sunday tea.

Gran said: 'If she's coming for her tea tomorrow she wants to tell her. If she doesn't, I will.' My mother interpreted this fairly intelligently and said: 'I'm going to tell her, don't you fret yourself.' She slid off down a chuntering landslide of recrimination until the old man, reverting to the main theme, came back with the heavy artillery.

'He's not bloody well old enough to stay out half the night, I've told him before. He can start coming in of a night, or else go and live somewhere else.

Boredom with Job
(101) (87)
Giving himself status

P10] Danny Boon   P27 cabinet
P34] Duxbry
35]

Lying to get out jam

p 59   p29
P34
p109

Thrill of playing a part
p13
p22

Deceiving his girl friends
_____

world of his

own

96
85/86 orchestra